Issue 26

Resisting Neo-liberalism

Soundings

SUBSCRIPTIONS
2004 subscription rates are (for three issues):
UK: Institutions £70, Individuals £35
Rest of the world: Institutions £80, Individuals £45

ISSN 1362 6620
ISBN 0 85315 993 9

Printed in Great Britain by
Cambridge University Press, Cambridge

Soundings is published three times a year, in autumn,
spring and summer by:
Soundings Ltd c/o Lawrence & Wishart,
99a Wallis Road, London E9 5LN.
Email: soundings@l-w-bks.demon.co.uk

Website: www.lwbooks.co.uk/sounding.html

CONTENTS

———————— Continued on next page ————————

Continued from previous page

NOTES ON CONTRIBUTORS

Katharine Ainger is co-editor of *New Internationalist* magazine.

Geoff Andrews is Lecturer in Politics at the Open University and a member of the *Soundings* editorial group. His book: *Not a Normal Country: Italy Under Berlusconi* will be published at the end of the year.

John Cowley is a writer and a lecturer in sociology at City University, London.

Cynthia Cockburn is a professor in the department of Sociology at City University, London and co-editor (with Dubravka Zarkov) of *The Postwar Moment* (L&W 2002).

Jane Foot is a freelance policy advisor, and researcher in community involvement.

Elizabeth Foy worked in the arts for fifteen years and is now training to be an Anglican priest.

Judy Gahagan is a psychologist turned writer, translator, poet. Currently, she teaches courses in archetypal and eco-psychology for poets, for the Poetry School. Her latest collection of poems is *Night Calling* (Enitharmon, 2003).

Jeremy Gilbert teaches Cultural Studies at the University of East London. Publications include Timothy Bewes & Jeremy Gilbert (eds) *Cultural Capitalism: Politics After New Labour* (L& W 2000).

Stuart Hall is a member of the *Soundings* editorial group and Emeritus Professor of Sociology at the Open University.

Clare Joy works for the World Development Movement.

Sayeed Khan is a journalist, lecturer and peace activist.

Ruth Levitas is Professor of Sociology at the University of Bristol. Her publications include *The Concept of Utopia* (1990); *The Inclusive Society?: Social Exclusion and New Labour* (1998; second edition forthcoming 2005); and, as co-editor with David Gordon and Christina Pantazis of *Poverty and Social Exclusion in Britain: The Millennium Survey* (Policy Press, forthcoming).

Jo Littler teaches Media and Cultural Studies at Middlesex University. She is currently co-editing a book with Roshi Naidoo entitled *The politics of heritage: the legacies of 'race'* (Routledge, forthcoming 2004).

Lorraine Mariner works at the Tate Gallery and Archive. Her poems have appeared in a number of magazines.

Doreen Massey is a member of the *Soundings* editorial group and Professor of Geography at the Open University.

Catherine Needham is a lecturer in Politics at Queen Mary, University of London, and a Research Associate for Catalyst.

Mario Petrucci won the Arvon poetry competition in 2002 and recently received an Arts Council/London Arts Board award. His new collection, *Heavy Wate*, will be published by Enitharmon in 2004.

Sylvie Prasad is a photographer, and a lecturer in media production at the University of East London.

Michael Rustin is a member of the *Soundings* editorial group and Professor of Sociology at the University of East London.

Debbie Shaw is a lecturer in Cultural Studies at the University of East London, who loves dogs.

Taking on neo-liberalism

The bulk of this issue of *Soundings* is given over to our ongoing critique of neoliberalism and New Labour, but there is a new emphasis in many of the articles on what our political response should be to the entrenched nature of Blairism. Especially since London will be playing host to the European regional gathering of the World Social Forum in November 2004, we want to address questions of how we can actively oppose neo-liberalism (of course trying to analyse what forces are in play is one of the ways in which we do this).

For some contributors - most notably Jeremy Gilbert - there is no point in trying to persuade New Labour to change course. Jeremy argues that the analysis carried in *Soundings* and elsewhere has made it abundantly clear that New Labour is a neoliberal hegemonic project, and as such there can be no point in persuading them to think about alternative forms of social democracy. (Ruth Levitas also cogently makes the case for New Labour's total lack of interest in social democracy of any kind, and shows how the deep is the immersion in New Labour double talk of some of those who are trying to criticise the government.) For Jeremy, this means that initiatives such as Compass have missed the point. It is time to turn away from Labour and begin to organise active opposition. Critics within the Labour Party could be allies in such opposition, but they would have to be much clearer than currently about the nature of New Labour, and committed to much stronger opposition than has been so far been evident. The attempt to win small concessions - something that so often seems to bog down the trade union movement - is no substitute for campaigning for a complete change of direction. One could take issue with some of Jeremy's tactical recommendations, but his argument that we are nowhere without popular movements of resistance is timely.

Our roundtable discussion addresses the question of how to resist neoliberal globalisation from the point of view of looking at the connections between the global and the local. The contributors ask how we might organise politically to take account of the global influences on local places, but also the influence of the local on the global. They look at some of the groups and campaigns that have been participating in the social forum movement and at some of the issues this kind of campaigning raises. For example, many popular or local movements have resisted aspects of corporate globalisation, but how can they make links with each other?; how do they relate to institutions of power (if at all)?; how can a sense of one's own place from which one resists also encompass a welcoming of diversity or adventure? These are all issues to which we plan to return.

Martin McIvor, in a short comment in response to some of the debates we have been carrying, points out that critical voices in the Labour Party are increasingly concerned about the government's lack of progress on what have hitherto been taken to be fairly non-controversial social democratic criteria - such as income equality and the health of the public realm. And he rightly argues the need for bridges between these voices and the new protest movements - and that any such dialogue would be greatly assisted by a more vibrant shared left culture. We are hoping that *Soundings* will play a role in developing this - in its discussions about the nature of New Labour and the global forces of neoliberalism, in helping to mobilise opposition and to provide a non-sectarian forum for thinking about how to effect change, and also in continuing to think about the politics that is everywhere in cultural life.

Thus in this issue, as well as the discussions on movements, we also continue our focus on resisting New Labour's ideological attack on the public sphere - in Catherine Needham's exploration of the effects of turning us all into customers, and in Mike Rustin's critique of dominant systems of public service audit. Mike's article is interesting in that it moves beyond critique to propose more constructive forms of inspection; this is a useful example of looking for places where the contradictions in public policy open up opportunities for contestation on the ground; engaging in a contestation about the ideas underlying a policy can then lead to alternatives being offered that have the potential to attract sufficient support to win change. Such strategies for change within institutions should be seen as complementary to other oppositional strategies.

Jo Littler's article on celebrity and meritocracy shows how popular culture helps to reproduce competitive individualism in its celebration of success, and of conspicuous consumption by the successful. This theme of popular culture and its role as a public sphere through which hegemonic and counter-hegemonic values are in play is discussed by Jonathan Rutherford in the second part of this editorial. Jonathan and Jo are addressing another aspect of *Soundings* - our effort to think about politics through culture. This is a crucial part of the process of strengthening a common popular democratic culture.

We close with a tribute to one of the greatest public intellectuals of the twentieth century - Edward Said, a man for whom culture, theory and action were inseparable.

SD

COMMENTARY

Common life

The detective stories of Swedish writer Henning Mankell depict a hard working policeman, Kurt Wallander, recently divorced, struggling to come to terms with his middle age, and worrying over the dog days of social democracy. Faced with serial killers, organised crime and an increasingly commercialised society, his thoughts drift to a foreboding about the future: 'more and more people are being judged to be useless and flung to the margins of society'. How will he deal with the great uneasiness he feels at these changes?

I was half way through reading the fourth Wallander book when I visited the National Gallery to look at recent work by the American video artist Bill Viola. Viola is preoccupied with the kind of questions which punctuate Wallander's life: 'what is happening to us?', 'what kind of world is this?'. He tackles the big issues of the body, emotions, life and death. Over the years, Viola has produced some poignant images, which puzzle over issues of birth and mortality, and he has found a growing audience amongst the younger educated metropolitan middle classes, who are looking for a sense of meaningfulness in their lives but who hold little sympathy for organised religion.

Viola avoids the obfuscations of religious faith to present us with a kind of sacred humanism. In his latest work actors mime scenes from mediaeval religious paintings, expressing a range of emotions - anguish, joy, despair, sorrow. But the images seem contrived and unconvincing, exuding a specific white American, middle-class sensibility. As an interpretation of the human condition in all its diversity they fall short. Viola appears unable to imagine other worlds beyond his own.

Soundings is a journal of politics, but one which recognises that people do not live by politics alone (certainly as it is normally understood). There are other questions that need asking, about ethics, about how we might live in relation to others and to society. Emile Durkheim described sacred things as being collective ideals that have fixed themselves on material objects, ideas and representations awakened in us by the spectacle of society. For Kurt Wallander, Sweden's social democratic traditions once provided this function. But his awareness of change, permeable borders, and the growing numbers of refugees, takes him in a different direction from Viola's righteous, conflict-free depiction of life. Wallander's disorientation and lack of answers are expressed in his memory of his dead colleague Rydberg. Confronted with an apparently insoluble crime, he wonders what words of advice his friend might have given - 'though knowing, even as he thinks this, that Rydberg too would be confounded by the new social realities'.

Faced with the spectacle of changing society, the left is confronted with a similar predicament. Where and what are the collective ideals? In societies which mistrust universal moralities, how are we to organise a democratic life which can manage both personal fulfilment and our obligations toward others? Singular explanatory narratives are proving to be very elusive. As Zygmunt Bauman has argued, these undecideables militate against simple solutions of for and against: 'They put paid to the ordering power of the opposition, and so to the ordering power of the narrators of the opposition. Oppositions enable knowledge and action, undecideables paralyse them.'[1]

There is no better example of the consequences of this paralysis than New Labour's embrace of the market. As if aware of its moral emptiness, Tony Blair's language, confronted by a world that he sees as 'changing at a bewildering speed', is filled with the need to hurry. 'There are no prizes for standing still', 'we cannot be complacent or rest on our laurels', 'we need continually to revise and revitalise our thinking'. Politics is about values that will 'drive us forward'. These values are 'progressive politics', 'providing economic opportunity', 'a modern civic society', 'a modern welfare state'. Modernise, progress, new, change, reform:

---

1. Zygmunt Bauman, *Modernity and Ambivalence*, Polity Press 1991, p56.

single words are joined up into catch-phrases - 'progressive renewal', 'renewing progressive politics', 'a new modern vision'. In the end, despite Blair's insistence that 'ideas are more important than ever', policy has become depoliticised and reduced to the technocratic functionalism of 'what works'.

Consequently, New Labour lacks a narrative to explain itself by; instead it parades before us a series of projects and initiatives which demonstrate that something is happening. For example, when he opened the Bexley Business Academy in Kent in 2003, Blair challenged critics of his reforms to come and look at the new school. The prestigious building was designed by Norman Foster, to criteria pioneered by education company 3Es, and with £2million in sponsorship from Sir David Garrard of property company Minerva plc. Garrard's image takes pride of place on the Business Academy website. The Academy is an International Baccalaureate Organisation World School - this is no bog-standard comprehensive. It is Blair's bold vision of what works. But this kind of project amounts to little more than expensive tinkering; and the public private partnerships involved in the setting up of City Academies merely create one-off opportunities for corporate philanthropy, and launch-pads for business interest in public sector services markets. And it is a kind of tinkering that fuels inequality, and distracts attention from the long-term decline in UK levels of public investment. Labour need more than this to address people's concerns about the future, and to find a language that imagines how we can all live together.

Paradoxically, this mixture of utilitarianism, liberal economics and the pursuit of the new has meant that New Labour now resembles more closely than any other political tradition that of nineteenth century whiggery. New Labour likes to describe itself as heir to the social liberalism of the Edwardian era - somewhere on the spectrum between the Liberal Asquith and the Socialist Keir Hardie. But this government has cast aside most of the history of labour politics, and has slid even further back in time. As with the Whigs, the championing of new markets and modernity is accompanied by a blind faith in their principal drivers - individual economic freedom and the accumulation of capital. The Whigs also saw science and enlightenment as co-existing quite easily with the colossal country estates of the rich, and the workhouses for the masses. As Karl Polanyi writes, this was an age in which the running of society was an adjunct of the market. 'Instead of economy being embedded in social relations, social relations are embedded in the economic system'.[2] Echoes of this can be heard in Gordon Brown's enthusiasm for a post-welfare, enterprise culture. He told the CBI 2001 conference:

> I want every young person to hear about business and enterprise in school, every college student to know there are opportunities in business, every teacher to be able to communicate the virtues of enterprise ... so encouraging a stronger pro-business, pro-enterprise, pro-wealth creating environment in our country.

New Labour has abandoned the idea of the public good. It has been seduced by the idea that neo-liberalism promotes individual choice. Its rhetoric can at times appear to mirror the individual struggle to create a personal identity - which has become the defining paradigm of how we live in Western cultures: we are called upon to invent our own identity and live in our own way and be true to ourselves. Yet to view the individual pursuit of self fulfilment and self determination as an individualised project subject only to rules of just conduct is mistaken. For individual identity expresses our two greatest - and incompatible - wants in life: freedom *and* security. We desire to experience our individual life as unique and meaningful to ourselves, but we equally feel a need to belong to, and define ourselves through, broader collectives. It is in our relationships with others - in what is constituted as the social - that we attempt to reconcile this paradox and make a sense of self that feels authentic. The intellectual poverty of neo-liberalism lies in its failure to recognise that individuals cannot be reduced to Homo Economicus. We are social and emotional beings and we need public discourses and spaces which can orchestrate, enable and symbolise commonalities which are the necessary framework for creating social cohesion and individual identity.

In the last decade new national and global public spaces have emerged which have enabled individuals to encounter one another in shared activity. Some have been very large: celebrations of the royal family; the countryside alliance march; the anti war demonstrations; England's rugby team victory. The anti-globalisation demonstrations mark an international collective oppositional

---

2. Karl Polanyi, *The Great Transformation*, Beacon Press, 1957, p57.

politics to corporate capitalism. And reality TV shows like *Pop Idol* and *Big Brother* have revitalised virtual communities of TV watchers. These public spectacles frequently engage with moral debates, preoccupations with identity, social tolerance, and the political meaning of civic life.

What's more, reality TV often reveals a liberal public response. Michelle McManus, the 15-stone winner of *Pop Idol*, and Alex Parks, the young 'out' lesbian who won the 2003 *Fame Academy*, were supported by a public that is willing to think about difference and vote for it. Similarly, the most recent series of *Wife Swap* - for all the manipulation that was employed to make for entertaining TV - was a fascinating insight into contemporary gender relations, adult relationships with children and the democratising of family life.

P opular culture and mass public gatherings are assiduously cultivated by commercial interests and the right-wing press, which downplay their more radical and challenging elements. But New Labour, despite being progressive on many social issues, has not cultivated these elements to shape an alternative hegemony of the public, one that is open, outward-looking and tolerant. On the contrary, on key (conservative) issues such as crime and punishment, asylum and tax, it has promoted an idea of the public inherited from Thatcherism. New Labour strategist Phillip Gould has described himself as a populist: 'Any progressive party and progressive government should listen to the voice of the people ... Labour is a people's party and the people's voice should be heard (*Guardian*, 24.8.99). But Gould's concept of the people appears to be a product of his own imagination, mixing his childhood memories with New Labour's disciplinary and utilitarian approach to modernisation. New Labour has fabricated a parochial, culturally conservative, homogeneous and self-absorbed public - one that has been privatised and left prone to fear, xenophobia and insecurity.

We need a different approach to popular politics - and here Hannah Arendt's notion of a common world is useful. In Arendt's account, we are born into a common world:[3] 'It transcends our lifespan into past and future alike; it was there before we came and will outlast our brief sojourn in it. It is what we have in common not only with those who live with us, but also with those who were

---

3. Hannah Arendt, *The Human Condition*, The University of Chicago Press, 1998, Chapter 2.

here before and with those who will come after.' But this historical collective sense of a common life can only survive to the extent it appears in public. Public life is where our specific individuality and locatedness is recognised; it is where we see 'sameness in utter diversity'. And, as Arendt argues: 'the privation of privacy lies in the absence of others', and is the cause of the 'mass phenomenon of loneliness'. The public realm is a gift of history, and a crucial task of a broad left popular politics is to recover it and articulate an idea of a common life and its sometimes incommensurable diversity.

Arendt's argument raises the question of ethics, since ethical life begins the moment we encounter others who are not reducible to ourselves, and realise that we must negotiate living in the world with them. Politics should not be confused with ethics. It is about compromise, negotiation, and hard decisions about the instrumental distribution of resources. But we need a democratic left politics which offers ways of articulating an ethics of commonality whose truths are the same for all. One which aspires to uphold individual integrity and a commonwealth of difference. The point of democratic participation is to create, rather than discover, common goods.

This is a task that the left in Britain has been tardy about addressing. A recent essay by *Prospect* editor David Goodhart - a self professed member of the liberal intelligentsia - is a dispiriting reminder of this timidity.[4] Goodhart argues that the growing diversity of British society (by which he means ethnic difference) is undermining its social cohesion and the values of solidarity which underpin the welfare state. Tellingly, his definition of the problem is borrowed from a Conservative politician, David Willets: 'The basis on which you can extract large sums of money in tax and pay it out in benefits is that most people think that the recipients are people like themselves, facing difficulties that they themselves could face. If values become more diverse, if lifestyles become more differentiated, then it becomes more difficult to sustain the legitimacy of a universal risk-pooling welfare state. People ask: "Why should I pay for them when they are doing things that I wouldn't do"'. Instead of rejecting this myth of an ahistorical, homogeneous, conflict-free national community, Goodhart, like New Labour, succumbs to it.

He justifies his argument by defining citizenship as not simply an abstract

---

4.   David Goodhart, 'Discomfort of Strangers', *The Guardian*, February 24 , 2004.

idea of rights and obligations, but as something that 'we' are born into: 'When politicians talk about the "British people" they refer ... to a group of people with a special commitment to one another'. His romanticised image of national community distracts attention from the one group who are guilty of breaking with the values of solidarity - the wealthy. It is the rich who exclude themselves from paying taxes and who are increasingly opting out of all forms of collective social provision. In Britain, it is class inequality, not racial differences, that threaten the fabric of society and notions of solidarity.

However the left cannot evade the issue of racism if it is to successfully revive the idea of the public good. Each of us is born with a past, and the stories of our lives are partly the stories of the communities from which we derive our identity. We are part of history and the bearers of a tradition. But as the philosopher Alasdair MacIntyre persuasively argues, we are not bound by their moral and political limitations. They are the places from which we begin and from where we move forward. Our personal aspirations and engagement with others change our identities and the traditions we have grown from. As MacIntyre argues: 'Traditions, when vital, embody continuities of conflict. When a tradition becomes unchanging and fixed, it is always dying or dead.'[5]

JR

---

5.   Alasdair MacIntyre, *After Virtue*, Duckworth 1999, p222.

How you can support

Soundings

We have now published 25 issues of *Soundings*, and we believe that the time is ripe to relaunch the journal. There is an acute need on the left for a forum for radical and open minded thinking. *Soundings* has begun this task, and we now have a renewed editorial collective whose aim is to bring an extra edge and focus to the *Soundings* project, so that it can become a major intellectual resource for the left.

Of course such a project needs funding and energy. So we are calling on our subscribers and supporters to help us. We are launching an appeal for investment, to fund a major promotions drive, and investment in improved production values and press work. We also would welcome volunteers to help on production and promotion.

You can help us by

- Subscribing to the journal
- Getting your institution to subscribe
- Sending money into the appeal
- Volunteering time
- Joining the *Soundings* email list and supporting *Soundings* events

---

Please send your donations to: **Soundings Appeal**

Lawrence and Wishart, PO Box 7701, Latchingdon, Chelmsford, CM3 6WL
Tel: 01621 741607 Fax: 020 8533 7369

To subscribe or to get your institution to subscribe, contact subs@lwbooks.co.uk

To go on the Soundings *email list, to receive information about* Soundings *events, please email sally@lwbooks.co.uk*

The New Labour debate

We publish below five more short commentaries on New Labour, following on from the debate initiated in Soundings 25. We asked contributors what they thought were the causes of New Labour's having lost its way, and what might constitute the basis for a new political direction for the British left. We also publish a response by Richard Minns to Geoff Andrews's editorial on New Labour in Soundings 25. We welcome contributions to the debate - please send any further comments to sally@lwbooks.co.uk.

Martin McIvor

The immediate challenge for the British left emerged clearly from the discussion in the last issue of Soundings. *There is a dilemma about where its bases for renewal truly lie. On the one hand, we have seen new waves of energetic and creative grassroots activism, geared primarily to international issues of corporate and military power such as anti-imperialism, the environment, and global economic justice. On the other hand, the Labour Party is now entering a period of flux - as questions are asked by increasing numbers of its members, affiliates and politicians about the government's lack of progress on standard social democratic success measures such as income equality and the health of the public realm. These parallel processes could reinforce and fruitfully feed off one another - the new protest movements are still limited in their reach and are not yet speaking clearly to the broad public that largely shares their concerns, while those searching for a post-Third Way agenda for Labour badly need to reconnect with the kind of political creativity and radical social critique that we see out on the streets. But right now they seem to be taking place in two totally separate worlds. Certainly the two moments should never be reduced to one another and they will never be wholly merged into any singular political project (though there will be points at which they need to interlock practically, and the trade unions will be one of the crucial bridges here). But both should be taking place within a shared left culture that can provide the right kind of communication channels* and transmission belts between them. *This will require a regrouping of the intellectual left in Britain - various currents that came out of the 1980s seem to have formed into isolated pools (in academia, or single-issue organisations, or on the 'hard' left, or advising the government) and they need to flow together again. A journal like Soundings has a very important role to play in this. An early task will be to sort out our thinking about 'social democracy'. For anyone inspired by 'new left' critiques of the post-war consensus, the felt need now to defend its institutions against the ongoing process of neo-liberal restructuring can be disorienting and dispiriting. But we must look for what is living and what is dead in these institutions, and be clear that the alternative we forge is no recovery or reversal, but emerges directly from the contemporary failings of the market society and the social resistance and opposition it is today generating.*

Natasha Grzincic

New Labour lost its way? No way - this is the path it has always intended and we're fools if we are still waiting for that glorious U-turn. New Labour's modernising agenda is only now being fully exposed, thanks to the failings of missionary Blair: the gleam in his eye when he says he's 'doing the right thing' no longer carries conviction - the majority of public and parliamentary opinion is now against him (on Iraq, tuition fees, foundation hospitals, to name the issues of the day).

The British left needs to put together an alternative that channels the energy of the new generation of activists that has emerged out of the anti-war and global justice movements. These new activists don't know where to go - but they definitely won't join the Labour Party en masse, whose leaders stabbed them in the back. And they're scared off by the seemingly omnipresent recruiters from the various revolutionary parties, many of whom appear to have little respect for democracy.

This alternative involves recognising the degree of unity that has grown up across the left, within and outside the labour movement, on democracy, public services, anti-racism and peace. It may take years of patient campaigning and open discussion to overcome distrust at the grassroots level and build new structures from the bottom-up - as it did in Scotland. The question then becomes, does George Galloway's Respect coalition fulfil these criteria?

Neil Jameson

History should have taught us that it is a myth that by simply changing one leader for another then all is well. There is a crisis in politics and public life today, but I do not believe that this is in any way caused by Tony Blair - it is a cop-out to lay everything on him, just as the left used to do on Margaret Thatcher, etc, etc. The crisis is mainly of our own making, and the increasingly sophisticated operation of the global market and its image-makers and story-tellers. We deny we have any power or responsibility for anything, and the market endorses this and then teaches us the lie that the mess is never our fault but that of one person - whoever happens to be in charge at Westminster at the time! For the last fifteen years, The Citizen Organising Foundation and our affiliate bodies like TELCO in East London have been challenging this superficial approach to politics and change. It is our daily experience that it is in the struggle to seek and achieve the common good that we find ourselves, and hopefully our neighbours. COF supports grass roots power alliances - faith groups, trade unions, student groups and schools, as we try to reclaim the power we have given away to corporations, bureaucrats, journalists and other similar elites. Broad-based community organising gives people a real and regular experience of politics, through actions and campaigns which address many of the grievances of communities with little power and even less money. TELCO's pioneering 'Living Wage' campaign has proved that it is possible for organised local communities to challenge both the greed of the market and the indolence of government. Westminster politics is enhanced by a strong and active civil society - that is where the left should be putting its efforts and energy today - just as it did at the beginning of the last century.

Zoe Williams

I have rather lost interest in Blair's future, as anything more than a curiosity - politically, his pursuit of triangulation has amounted to pragmatic conservatism, and his desire for a third-term is only interesting on a psychological level, and then only mildly. My hopes for the left come from a remark Howard Dean made during his campaign - that he was seeking not to filch votes from existing parties, but get his support from the 50 per cent of Americans who currently don't vote. Refusing to vote has traditionally been seen as a sign of indifference and/or apathy, but in these third-way conditions it is a concrete political statement. It says: 'these parties are not dissimilar enough; I refuse to ally myself to any of them, or legitimise them with my vote'. And in so doing, I think it radicalises outside runners, since it gives them a credible hope that, contrary to what the media would have us believe, not everybody adheres to the basic tenets of modern governance (in a nutshell: capitalism, unavoidable; redistributive taxation, passé). I would actively champion non-voting as a strategy for the next election, since the larger this untapped constituency is, the sooner we'll have a innovative outsider of our own to champion.

Alan Hooper

Is there a future for the left-socialist and 'anti-capitalist' - beyond New Labour? Is it possible to identify the features of a new political movement which could begin to mount a credible alternative to Blairism or Brownism come to that? The first requirement surely is to resolve what might be called the Miliband dilemma: should the left be in or out - some of course want to be both - of the Labour Party? This question has bedevilled socialists at least since the 1920s, but I believe an answer has now been provided for us by Blair and the New Labour project during the last decade. Blair has shifted the political balance of Labour decisively towards the first part of Lenin's famous couplet: Labour is now a bourgeois party, like the US Democrats. Moreover, in its actions and in its convictions it is an anti-working-class party, neo-liberal in its economic agenda and neo-imperialist in its international allegiances. Good people remain in the Labour Party but socialists should be outside, asserting the necessity and possibility of an alternative. Their motto: on s'engage et puis on voit.

A response to 'Rocky Times', *Soundings* Issue 25

Geoff Andrews kicked off the debate about the 'way' for Labour, or Labour losing its 'way', by suggesting that 'one defining "transformist moment" in the reorientation of Labour had been the abandonment of the *Commission on Social Justice Report* (CSJ), set in train by the late John Smith. 'The CSJ,' Geoff writes, 'was an attempt to provide a modern social democratic response to a new era of welfare and education … It took a holistic, modern and innovative approach to the welfare state, one that was rooted in the traditions of the left' (p10). There are many concepts here begging further analysis, but for the sake of brevity what 'traditions on the left' did CSJ embody? A look at this helps us to identify defining moments and the 'way' Labour has developed.

The CSJ outlook was rooted in its selection of one from three broad strategic choices These choices were caricatured as 'Investors', 'Deregulators', and 'Levellers'. 'Investors' (the CSJ preferred choice) achieve security, economic and social justice by redistributing opportunities. 'Deregulators' (the Tories) undermine security in order to achieve economic success. The 'Levellers' (presumably 'old' Labour) distribute wealth to the neglect of its production. They aim for redistribution through the benefits system, 'rather than through a new combination of active welfare state, reformed labour market, and strong community' (CSJ, Verso 1994, p96).

The implication is that the 'Levellers' are well-intentioned myopic dreamers, out of touch with 'modern' 'reality', or the quest for economic growth. 'Theirs is a strategy for social justice based primarily on redistributing wealth and incomes, rather than trying to increase opportunities and compete in world markets' (p96). Call me old-fashioned, but I thought that the former was exactly what Labour was supposed to be about.

So, for example, increasing the old age pension in line with earnings, as articulated by pensioners' movements and as won as a policy at a Labour national conference and then ignored, must on these criteria be a Levellers' policy. Indeed, the CSJ preferred arrangement for pensions (presumably an 'Investor' strategy) was as follows, albeit with some ambivalence and qualifications:

♦ It proposed a means-tested 'pension guarantee' - increasing the basic state pension across the board was considered too expensive.
♦ It considered that private funding of pensions might increase savings and investment.[1]
♦ It proposed individualisation of pension provision through privatisation, arguing that introducing more self-reliance was better than promising ourselves higher pensions on the assumption that future generations would pay (p279). Private funding was regarded as superior because it creates individual 'ownership rights'.[2]

All these recommendations are now New Labour policies. And they have in

---

1. For a refutation of this position see my 'Pensions of mass destruction', in *Soundings* 24.
2. As also argued in 'Pensions of mass destruction', this kind of approach undermines intergenerational solidarity (community) in favour of greater individual ownership of personal property rights - it advocates personal ownership claims as opposed to community entitlement and sharing.

the course of time wrecked pension provision in the UK, while producing no increase in savings and investment.

So, the 'transformist moment' (if indeed there was such a moment) was not, as Geoff implies, a rejection of the CSJ. The current way forward for Labour was endorsed by the publication of the CSJ, with its carefully crafted introduction of 'newness' into its title - *Social Justice: Strategies for National Renewal*. Those who are now disappointed with New Labour should not be surprised. It was unlikely to be any other 'way'. The CSJ told you so.

Contributors

Natasha Grzincic is Deputy Editor of *Red Pepper*; **Alan Hooper** teaches politics at London Metropolitan University; **Neil Jameson** is Executive Director COF and Lead Organiser with London Citizens; **Martin McIvor** is Director of the left think tank Catalyst (www.catalystforum.org.uk), and was a contributor to the recent 'Compass' statement; **Richard Minns** is the author of *The Cold War in Welfare; Stock Markets versus Pensions*, Verso, 2001; **Zoe Williams** is a columnist on *The Guardian*.

The second wave

The specificity of New Labour neo-liberalism

Jeremy Gilbert

Jeremy Gilbert argues that all the talk about persuading New Labour to rethink is hopeless optimism, and that the only way to oppose its wholehearted embrace of neo-liberalism is to build popular opposition to the government, and to the global forces to which it is linked.

The other 1997

If May 1997 was a missed opportunity, it was not only because of the subsequent direction of the current government. As Stuart Hall points out in his characteristically expert analysis ('New Labour's Double-Shuffle', *Soundings* 24), even before the 1997 election it appeared clear that New Labour had decided to pursue a neo-liberal agenda. Beyond this, there now seems little reason to believe that there was any real chance of a government elected at that moment implementing a socially progressive programme. This was not only apparent in the policy documents and political statements of New Labour leaders. It was always going to be the case at that moment that the pressures on any incoming administration to implement neo-liberal policies were likely to be far greater than any obvious countervailing force. With the trade union movement exhausted, the organised left in disarray and the new political movements hopelessly disorganised, unclear about their real potentialities and lacking effective strategies, there was never much likelihood of the government acting in any way other than as it has done. The neo-liberal agenda of the US, and the lack of effective resistance to it throughout the world, the success of capital in completely dissolving the civil society of the former Soviet Union and Yugoslavia, and the complete failure of the Western European powers to prevent this, surely made apparent the pressures which would be felt by any incoming regime to commit to a neo-liberal ideal of 'modernisation'. To think otherwise is to put an incredible faith in the power of governments to act alone and change the world. To put this point very simply: progressive policies have never, anywhere in the world, been implemented by governments who were not backed and/or pressured by strong and well-organised popular movements demanding such change. It was the absence of any such movement, not simply the contingent decisions of a handful of individuals close to the Labour leadership, which made the neo-liberal direction of this government already inevitable in 1997.

From this perspective also, however, May 1997 did represent a historic missed opportunity for the British left. For much of the early 1990s, the political energies of a new generation of activists had been focused on the radical environmentalism of the anti-roads movement and associated campaigns around housing, the environment, freedom of association, etc. It is often forgotten now, but this movement scored some spectacular victories, winning widespread sympathy across a range of social constituencies, and effectively achieving its immediate goal of making the government's extensive road-building plan so expensive and so unpopular as to be untenable. Those plans were shelved indefinitely in the mid-1990s, awaiting John Prescott's tenure at the Department of Environment for them to be fully reinstated. Having developed largely in isolation from the labour movement and the organised left, it had often seemed unlikely that participants in this movement could ever work alongside members of more traditional organisations. However, May 1997 saw the culmination of the 'Reclaim the Future' project to build an alliance between the new direct-action politics and radical trade unionists supporting the sacked Liverpool dock workers. The result was an enormous (by the standards of the time) demonstration to Trafalgar square on 1 May, involving for the first time both significant numbers of activists associated with projects like Reclaim the Streets and masses of trade unionists from around the country. In many ways this was RTS's finest moment: the group that pioneered the street party as a form of non-violent political protest managed to get a sound system into the road outside the National Gallery, filling its famous steps with dancers. The combined event became a mixture of free rave and traditional rally: trade unionists and Trotskyists listened to speakers from the conventional left while others danced in the sunshine. The potential for an alliance between the 'new' politics and the old felt palpable.

Or at least, it did for the first couple of hours. But once the rally had ended, and the many ravers and eco-protesters who had listened patiently to a tediously predictable set of speeches in support of the dockers went to join the dancing throng, something both disappointing and profoundly symbolic happened. The trade unionists, with a few bewildered and occasionally disgusted backward glances at the frivolity on the National Gallery steps, started to leave. Within an hour or so most of them had gone home. The momentary alliance had lasted for as long as the kids and crusties were prepared to participate on their terms, but the idea that any significant number of the leftists might join this particular kind of party was simply not on the agenda. Those left behind felt suddenly isolated, and we were. Immediately the trade union contingents had vacated the square, it was sealed off by police, who began a hostile set of manoeuvres intended exclusively to antagonise, intimidate and provoke the remaining protesters. The result: for the first time, Reclaim the Streets saw its name connected with a violent affray between protesters and police, rather than with the creative non-violence which had been its trademark up to that point.

I t was immediately after this that RTS, and the political formation to which it had become unwittingly central, shifted attention from the local, popular and winnable goal of forcing a change in the direction of UK transport policy, to the much more abstract objective of confronting 'capitalism' itself. There were a number of reasons for this. Some were quite sound: activists had an increasing sense of the global nature of the threat they faced, and a desire to act in solidarity with struggles such as the Zapatista movement and the North American anti-WTO campaign which culminated in the Seattle events. But others were ludicrous: most notably, the explicitly millenarian belief shared by key activists that there was only one small step from getting the Major government to postpone its road-building plan to successful world revolution against capitalism in all its forms. But for whatever the reason, this was in any meaningful political terms a disastrous move. RTS and the 'anti-capitalist' movement quickly lost the public support that they had built in the first part of the decade (to the delight of those anarchist sections to whom notoriety was always more important than actual social change). Capitalism appears now to have been quite untroubled by their efforts, and the road-building programme has been fully re-instated.

Precisely what the movement lacked at that crucial moment was any sense of the texture, the limitations and the potential of what Gramsci famously calls the 'national-popular': the site at which, within the socio-cultural context of the nation state, on the terrain of its everyday life, hearts and minds are won and lost. Substituting a language which had no resonance with the lives of most British people (the rhetoric of anti-globalisation) for one which had united sentiments from Glasgow to Middle England (the utopian environmentalism of the anti-car movement), they lost what little ground they had won in their 'war of position', and were forced back into an isolated trench, the political ghetto of hardcore anti-capitalist anarchism. But who could have given them such a sense? Who could have taught the practitioners of the new politics some hard-won lessons of the old? The labour movement of course. Instead, the labour movement looked away, mesmerised by the prospect of a Labour government, despite the fact that Blair had made absolutely explicit the limits of any co-operation he would be prepared to countenance with trade unions. *Red Pepper* aside, the remnants of the New Left expended their energy in horrified outrage that Blair had begun to do exactly what he had said he was going to do ever since being elected Labour leader.

The awful irony of this situation is that both the British labour movement and the intellectual-political current associated with *Soundings* could well have had something distinctive to learn from the direct-action movement at just this crucial juncture. It is precisely a recognition of the global nature of neo-liberalism and the necessity for opposition to it to be international in scope which has been the great strength of the anti-globalisation movement since 1997. Conversely, as Hall points out, the analysis of Thatcherism which has formed the basis for responses to New Labour in these pages was rather too focused on the dimension of the national-popular, overlooking the extent to which Thatcherism was one, very localised (and, I would add, short term) manifestation of global neo-liberalism.

So we have a situation, in 1997, in which, on the one hand, the labour movement and the intellectual legatees of the New Left were so focused on the nuanced specificities of national electoral politics that they appeared not to see either the inevitability of New Labour's commitment to neo-liberalism or the significance of the emerging international movement against it; and, on the other hand, that movement was itself incapable of operationalising its global analysis at the level of effective political strategy in the national-popular context. If there was ever a moment when it looked like things could have been different, it was 1 May 1997. As so often in the past, however, the cultural conservatism and political inertia of the British labour movement decided the outcome for the worse.

Two waves of neo-liberalism: from Thatcherism to New Labour

Hall is clearly right that the earlier analysis of Thatcherism underestimated the global nature of neo-liberalism, and theorised it somewhat too narrowly as a national formation. It seems remarkable now that the lessons coming from Mitterrand's France and Bob Hawke's Australia should have been so overlooked: in both cases, nominally social democratic governments were implementing economic policies typical of the Thatcher and Reagan administrations, and indeed of the Callaghan Labour government in the UK. Looked at in this international context, and in the light of subsequent history, it seems appropriate to re-designate Thatcherism as the specific national form which the first wave of neo-liberalism took in the UK, once the Labour government had proved politically incapable of sustaining the experiment in monetarism already begun by Dennis Healey in the second half of the 1970s - and not as the fundamental break in British political history that it is sometimes represented as being. Looked at in this light, however, Thatcherism is no less remarkable and distinctive - less 'epochal', in Hall's terms - as a political phenomenon. Indeed, as a hegemonic project it appears more impressive than ever. From this perspective, Thatcherism's successful articulation of neo-liberal economics with social conservatism was always a rather unlikely prospect; it succeeded in creating common ground between radically divergent social constituencies, and in alienating libertarians, liberals, socialists and social democrats - who between them have always made up a clear majority of British opinion - without ever uniting them in effective opposition to it. It was of course Hall himself who first analysed the contradictory logic of this articulation, and accurately predicted that it was this contradiction which would undermine Thatcherism amongst an increasingly liberal electorate.[1]

In this sense, it was always the cultural politics of Thatcherism, rather than its economic programme, which was distinctive, and which distinguishes it from the project of New Labour. New Labour's instincts have always been socially liberal. While there may have been a visible willingness to accommodate to conservative forces on headline-grabbing issues such as cracking down on asylum-seekers, its policies of putting single mothers to work, attacking racism in the police force (about which more later), gradually decriminalising recreational drugs, and equalising the age of consent for gay men, all manifest a socio-cultural project which in key ways is fundamentally at odds with that of Thatcherism. To dismiss such differences as merely cosmetic, as some commentators do, is to imply that only the economic programme of a government, party or movement actually determines its political character. This is clearly a mistake.

From a contemporary vantage point, it looks as if Thatcherism's specific articulation of social conservatism with neo-liberal economics confused many people, despite the best efforts of Hall et al to demystify it. One symptom of this confusion was the persistent belief in many left circles that Blair must be a fundamentally benign figure because of his evident commitment to certain kinds of social liberalism. He looked, in Hall's own words, 'like someone who would have a gay person to dinner', unlike Tory or Labour leaders of the past. As Hall and others pointed out, Thatcherism had effectively produced a 'chain of equivalence' between Englishness, neo-liberalism and social conservatism that was by no means inevitable at the end of the twentieth century. However, today one has the impression that this hegemonic linkage was so successful that many on the British left had themselves come to believe, by the middle of the 1990s, in its absolute inevitability: hence the genuine surprise expressed by so many since that time that Blair has turned out to be not 'really' a socialist or even a social democrat at all, despite being a liberal on social issues. Instead, Blair has attempted to re-articulate the elements of British political discourse, producing a new 'chain of equivalence' that links social liberalism, competitive individualism, neo-liberal economics and modernity itself.

---

1. Stuart Hall, *The Hard Road to Renewal*, Verso 1988.

And this has not turned out - as too many hoped for too long - to be a short term tactic, but is precisely the long-term strategy which he and other proponents of the Third Way always said it was. Blair always insisted he could be for gay rights and yet remain committed to neo-liberal economics. Confounding those who convinced themselves that he could not possibly have meant what he said, he has proved himself quite capable of doing exactly that.

Such confusion is symptomatic of the problems with the analysis of Thatcherism which Hall himself diagnoses. Underplaying the flexibility with which neo-liberalism was already accommodating itself to a range of different national-popular contexts, this analysis focused too much on the narrow

> 'Thatcherism might be said to have been at least as "hybrid" as New Labour'

British experience. Whatever the reasons for this, we might speculate now that the excessive focus on the specific national and party-political form of first-wave neo-liberalism, at the expense of an adequate attention to its international resonances and local cultural specificities, has resulted in a concomitant obsession with national and party-political sites of opposition to both first and second-wave neo-liberalism (or their absence). A fixation on parliamentary politics, and on the Labour Party and its failings, has all but obscured the significance of the emergent international opposition to neo-liberalism which the direct-action movement was the first to notice, and with which the UK labour movement has still signally failed to connect in any meaningful way. The one instance in which such connections have been made was in the recent campaign against the privatisation of IT services in Newcastle, led by Unison and explicitly linking its campaign to the global 'anti-capitalist' campaign against privatisation. And what do you know? That particular fight against privatisation was actually won.

This analysis complicates the status of Hall's claim that New Labour should be characterised as a hybrid formation: not because this is an inadequate description of New Labour - far from it - but rather because it is not clear that New Labour is any more 'hybrid' than Thatcherism was. Thatcherism might be said to have been at least as 'hybrid' as New Labour, with its appeals to social conservatism being a necessary and ongoing concession to those settled Middle English constituencies who were always going to have much to lose from the social dislocation brought about by advanced capitalism. These constituencies may not have lost as much as the Scottish, Welsh, and Northern English industrial workers, but neo-liberalism's capacity to undermine a world of settled social, ethnic and gendered relationships - disrupting forever the social hierarchies of the suburbs, the coherence of white England and that bedrock of bourgeois psychic life, 'the family' - always had the potential to provoke resistance amongst those constituencies which Thatcherism's social conservatism was aimed at keeping on-side. Such resistance is registered even today at the level of shared fantasy: it is not only the left-romantics of the environmental movement who have made *Lord of the Rings* - a work which is at root a colossal exercise in nostalgia, set in an imaginary Northern Europe in which the early middle-ages never gave way to the proto-modernity of the Renaissance - the most popular work of narrative fiction in English or any other language. This conservative constituency was never fully comfortable with Thatcher's instantly-regretted outburst that there was no such thing as society, conscious as it was that it is precisely 'Society' which tells gay men that they cannot marry, Rastafarians that they cannot smoke cannabis, and homeless people that they cannot sleep in our streets.

Ultimately, of course, just as Hall predicted in the 1980s, Thatcherism never was going to be able to hold back the tide of social transformation which its own version of untrammelled, 'disorganised' capitalism had unleashed. Seen in this light, the Major government's doomed 'back to basics' campaign can be seen as not merely an exercise in gross political incompetence, but as the inevitable last gasp of a project which had always been dependent upon such social conservatism for even its limited success. Indeed, Blair's early flirtation with communitarianism can be seen as a virtually seamless continuity with this strand of Thatcherism; it was not, as some hoped, a revival of ethical socialism, more a recognition of the continuing need to reassure those conservative constituencies alarmed by the social implications of neo-liberalism.

In these terms, we might well see the first three years of Blair and Brown's government as simply holding the Thatcherite course - putting the authoritarian Jack Straw in the home office and keeping to Tory spending plans - before finally moving the country into the second phase of full-scale marketisation. Indeed, it is worth reflecting at this point that, just as the Callaghan government fell because its ideological and political investment in Fordist social democracy rendered it incapable of implementing the industrial restructuring required by first-wave neo-liberalism, the Major government was ultimately undone because Thatcherism's ideological investment in English nationalism left it incapable of pushing through the next phase, to which globalisation in general and European integration in particular are as central as new forms of social liberalism. From this point of view, New Labour can be seen as a gang of technocrats hired by international capital to the job which Major - encumbered by the Little Englandism of his party - could not. That job involves opening up new British markets, and it is hard to see that happening outside of the context of further European integration. What results from this is precisely that more polite, more multicultural manner which distinguishes Blair from Thatcher, and which so bewitched the progressive intelligentsia for so long. We on the left may well find Blair's cosmopolitan capitalism more palatable than the vulgar xenophobia of Thatcher's preferred model, but we should never delude ourselves that it is any less integrated into the neo-liberal project. At the level of everyday life in the UK, it is its deep commitment to enforcing the norms of competitive individualism which makes this clear, as well as giving it such dangerous resonance with much of contemporary culture.

The hegemony of competitive individualism

By contrast with the 'mixed' Thatcherite project - which I am suggesting effectively remained in place from 1979 until about 2000 - New Labour's programme since 2000 (the time of the first Comprehensive Spending Review) is actually far more focused and consistent with a purely neo-liberal agenda. It is still an adaptation of the neo-liberal programme to specific historical conditions, but that adaptation is by nature rather less contradictory than Thatcherism's, precisely because Thatcherism had already cleared so much of the ground for it. As Alan Finlayson has pointed out, New Labour is simply opposed to anything and everything that stands in the way of the implementation of market relations across every possible social sphere.[2] This invaluable formulation enables us quite neatly to explain the apparent inconsistency in New Labour's deployment of its centralist, authoritarian instincts. Where resistance to the free flow of money or people, or to the full marketisation of

---

2. Alan Finlayson, *Making Sense of New Labour*, Lawrence & Wishart 2003; see also Finlayson's paper on http://www.signsofthetimes.org.uk/.

British and world society, is encountered, then the most brutal and arbitrary actions are justified. So those economic migrants who can be relied upon to behave as individualised economic actors, lowering the price of labour and contributing to the profitability of the economy, are implicitly tolerated or actively encouraged; while those who demand excessive levels of public support, who insist on bringing their families, cultures, and their archaically communal value-systems with them (these are the images which the term 'asylum seeker' is used to evoke) are to be excluded as violently as necessary. This commitment to the enforced implementation of individualised market relations is maintained even when, as in the case of differential tuition fees, it threatens the very future of the prime minister.

The form that this set of commitments most typically takes is that of a project to enforce competitive individualism as the paradigmatic mode of personal, social and institutional interaction. It is at this level that the Department of Education's implementation of standardised testing in schools goes hand-in-hand with the inexorable rise of celebrity culture. This is what accounts for the refusal of government to address the housing shortage in terms which do not regard the striking rise in single-person owner-occupancy - like the relentless rise in reliance on the private motor car - as both inevitable and desirable; and for the insistence that public service users behave as consumers in a buyers' market, always suspicious of the motives and competence of 'producers'. Across all of these sites an atomised individuality is not only encouraged: it is positively enforced by the active suppression of alternatives. Any form of life which depends on collectivity or communality of any kind is discouraged and rendered unviable.

This agenda will tend to manifest itself as socially liberal, even libertarian, except when faced with direct obstacles to its progress. One way of examining what is going on here is to consider the contemporary politics of policing. It is clear from recent events that the government, the higher echelons of the police, and the liberal journalistic establishment are all committed to driving old-fashioned forms of racism out of the police force. In the early days of Thatcherism, a brutally racist police force was a useful thing: only a force drawn exclusively from that section of the white working class which was committed to Thatcher's post-Powell anti-immigration stance could be relied upon to act as a political tool in the struggle against insurgent elements, from Brixton to the Northern coal fields. Contemporary neo-liberalism has no need for such an institution. Urban black communities have been ravaged and disrupted apparently beyond repair. The competitive individualism of contemporary black youth culture - a perpetual incitement to inter-communal violence and personal self-enrichment, rather than even symbolic opposition to political and economic oppression; a glorification of poverty and enforced criminality rather than a critique of it - disciplines that potentially unruly population more effectively than the police ever could. The unions have long since been broken, and amongst the Northern populations left behind by de-industrialisation, fascism and racism are embarrassing manifestations of a residual communalism which can only hold back the full dissemination of individualistic, entrepreneurial, cosmopolitan values. The problem is that the very history which has produced this situation has left behind a legacy of mistrust in the police across wide swathes of the public, such that, in the main, the only people who are now actually willing to join up are members of those residual white working-class communities amongst whom fascist and proto-fascist ideas fill the void left by the collapse of both Thatcherism and socialism. The result is the bizarre spectacle of the government, media and upper ranks going to great lengths to try to *discipline the police*: training schemes and internal investigations abound, as the government tries to instil *Guardian*-reader values into a *Sun*-reader police force, trying desperately and without much success to persuade them that they simply cannot arrest a man any more just because he is driving a car and is black. It is the very anxiety of the government when faced with the difficulty of using the police to enforce the normative codes of liberal individualism which demonstrates how deep their commitment to those codes goes. We should not mistake that commitment for any kind of sympathy with a wider social critique of racism and its sources, nor dismiss it as merely cosmetic. It is an enormous break with the legacy of Thatcherism, while being just as hostile to any form of socialist analysis or intervention as Thatcherism ever was. More than this, it is an approach which is ultimately *more* straightforwardly informed by that radical individualism which is the natural concomitant of neo-liberalism than was Thatcherism's contradictory, 'hybrid' articulation of neo-liberal economics, bourgeois individualism, and 'Victorian' social values.

Of course, as Hall so astutely points out, the government is forced into a pragmatic accommodation with a range of agendas, particularly to its left. Hall sees this in terms of New Labour possessing a 'subaltern' social democratic programme which is always subordinate to its dominant neo-liberal agenda. However, I am not sure that even the routine concessions which New Labour makes to a redistributive agenda can be consistently characterised as social democratic. Rather, the goal seems to be the implementation of that most individualistic of social values: meritocracy. New Labour is quite explicit in its commitment to the basic principle of meritocracy: equality of opportunity. At the same time, they deploy a range of disparaging epithets to distance themselves from any social democratic alternative to individualised, competitive meritocracy: most notably the notorious jibe at the expense of 'bog-standard comprehensives', and the caricature of social democracy as offering 'one-size fits all' solutions. The important point here is that this meritocratic agenda, unlike Thatcherism, does at times require the implementation of certain kinds of redistributive policy in order to create equality of opportunity: hence Gordon Brown's impressive personal campaign against child poverty. The trust funds to be established for new-born children are a perfect example of a wholly individualised policy with partially redistributive effects; but the social democratic goal of parity between the actual life experiences of citizens is not an intended effect of this policy at all. I would suggest that Brown's simultaneous support for this programme and for variable university tuition fees should not only be understood in terms of New Labour's 'mixed' agenda. Rather, both should be seen as entirely consistent with this meritocratic drive towards the full marketisation and individualisation of society. Where New Labour is opposed to social inequality - as in the case of children - it is only and precisely to the extent that such inequality is seen as an impediment to the efficient working of market mechanisms.

New Labour and post-democracy

Of course Hall is right that these redistributive measures must be 'spun' to social democratic constituencies as representing concessions to their interests, and he rightly draws our attention to the vacuity of New Labour's claim to be 'empowering communities' by reducing their relationship to essential services to that of individualised consumers. However, what I want emphasise here is the extent to which this is not merely a matter of 'spin'. In fact, this element of New Labour's politics possesses a high degree of internal consistency, and is implicitly informed by a very powerful argument, one which New Labour thinkers like Mulgan and Leadbeater were well on the way to formulating back when they were still writing for *Marxism Today*. The argument (which, of course, only a reckless narcissist like Peter Mandelson would ever risk making fully in public) goes something like this: representative democracy, mass participatory politics, and genuinely egalitarian social democracy are now historical artefacts. They belong, more-or-less exclusively, to the period of Fordist capitalism, which depended upon a higher level of social integration than any form of capitalism before or since. None of these institutions possesses the flexibility or dynamism to cope with the complexity of contemporary, postmodern societies, or to withstand the pressure of globalising capitalism and its corrosive flows. In this context we must accept that the only effective form of democracy is the market. Hence, only the marketisation of public services can hope to make them subject to any form of effective democratic accountability. In this new context, government will inevitably fall to technocratic elites who, if they are benign, will use the most powerful consultation techniques available (namely, those by which corporations consult their customers) to ensure that they give people more-or-less what they want, in so far as it in their power to do so. Beyond this, the most that government can do for its customer-citizens today is to equip them as best it can to survive in the harsh and competitive environment of the global labour-market. Old-fashioned ideas like holistic education or generous public pensions may exert a certain sentimental pull, but that only makes them all the more dangerous, as today these are untenable goals whose fruitless pursuit will only prevent us from adequately equipping our citizens to look after themselves in a world from which government cannot protect them. Students must follow degree programmes which make them attractive to employers. Citizens must save for their own futures, or perish. The Private Finance Initiative is the only way to increase investment in public services while maintaining any form of public accountability over them whatsoever, as direct investment by the treasury is simply not on the agenda; and the international pressure to privatise cannot be fully resisted without mass mobilisations of the kind seen in Bolivia, which we are simply not going to see on the streets of Basildon. This is the core argument in favour of what Anthony Barnett has called 'corporate populism',[3] the basis of what Finlayson calls the 'Schumpeterian workfare regime'.

---

3. See *New Left Review*, May/June 2000.

It is an argument which has tremendous resonance with the everyday lives of people who find Tesco and Amazon to be ever more responsive to their personal needs, and public services and government progressively less so.

The trouble with this argument is that it is right. Nothing that has happened anywhere in the world since 1973 offers serious evidence with which to contradict it. As Colin Crouch argues in a recent *Fabian Society* pamphlet, we are now living in the era of 'post-democracy', when voter turn-outs plummet, as electorates, explicitly or implicitly, realise that democracy simply does not work any more.[4] Governments do not merely pursue occasional unpopular policies: they pursue entire social agendas which their publics explicitly oppose. Even in Eastern Europe, where the euphoria of democratisation is still part of living memory, electoral participation rates are in free-fall. Taken in line with the accounts of postmodernity offered by commentators such as David Harvey, it now seems fair to say that effective representative democracy - which, broadly, forced governments to act in line with the express wishes of the electorate - was, like social democracy, a historical phenomenon specific to the moment of Fordist modernity. That era ended a generation ago.

O f course, much of this analysis will already be familiar to many readers of *Soundings*. It is essentially the 'New Times' critique of Labourism and existing social democracy made by Hall, Mulgan et al at the end of the 1980s. For thinkers such as Mulgan and Leadbeater, it provided the basis for their full endorsement of New Labour,[5] and something very like it is at the root of Anthony Giddens's advocacy of the Third Way. However, most of the authors of the New Times analysis never wanted or expected their ideas to become the basis for a second phase of neo-liberal government. Rather, they seem to have hoped that by charting the new terrain they would make possible the emergence of a new socialist project. This is where the crunch comes, however. Very little of the polemic, critique or thoughtful policy work produced by this intellectual current over the past ten years has actually engaged with the core elements of the New Labour argument. Most of it, like Hall's piece, seems to be predicated on the assumption that a New Labour government could have returned to an updated

---

4.   Colin Crouch, *Coping With Post-Democracy*, Fabian Society 2000.
5.   Hall & Jacques (eds), *New Times*, Lawrence & Wishart 1989.

version of social democracy - raising tax revenues, investing in public services, democratising the state - if it had really wanted to. But there is simply no evidence that this is the case. There is no evidence that major investment in public services, of the kind that the PFI is intended to generate, could occur in any other way without provoking a tax-payers' revolt. There is no evidence that any further democratisation of the local, national or regional state would not simply hand over power to extremists and random elements, given that the vast majority of the public show no interest in political participation at all. There is no evidence that the labour market could be more heavily regulated than it has been without producing the kind of economic downturn now being suffered in Germany, France and Japan.

What is the alternative?

Does this mean that I am about to advocate a full capitulation to the project of New Labour? It does not. But it does demonstrate, I think, that those of us who have always fully accepted the validity of Hall's analyses have at times been slow to appreciate the full implications of those perspectives. For surely, with the benefit of hindsight, they made clear all along that New Labour was the only place for the Labour leadership to go. The only other potential implication was for the Labour Party to transform itself into a socialist, New Left party, with a platform rather like that which the Green Party stands on today, conceding much of the political centre-ground to the liberal democrats, with whom it would have entered into a long-term political coalition. This was, in effect, the vision implicit in much of the advice offered by *New Statesman* and *Marxism Today* in the run-up to the 1987 and 1992 general elections. It might have taken Britain and the rest of Europe into a very different future, but it would have spelt the end of the dream of majority Labour government, and so was never going to happen in a million years as far as most Labour MPs were concerned. This is why the tone of much of the writing in *Soundings* and places close to it since then has seemed to me to be inappropriate. So much of it has amounted to attempts to reprove New Labour for getting it 'wrong' (as the cover of the 1998 special edition of *Marxism Today* put it), and to implore it to change direction, assuming that, fundamentally, Blair et al must still share our socialist values, and must not realise the full implications of what they are doing. They do, and what is more, they have a more consistent analysis of the current global situation and their role in it than has been offered by any of their half-hearted social democratic critics. One of the reasons Hall's article, like Rutherford's analysis of the 'market state' (*Soundings* 24), is so important is that it encourages us to acknowledge that this is not a contingent set of errors being made by New Labour, but a fully-fledged hegemonic project to which the left's only meaningful response can be opposition.

B ut what could such opposition look like? Is there only a meaningless choice to be made between begging the Labour leadership not to do exactly what the New Times analysis always implied it would have to do, and accepting the neo-liberal dictum that 'there is no alternative'? Of course not. If the past teaches us one thing, it is that there is always an alternative, the game is never over, and history never ends. Gramsci famously counsels us to temper 'pessimism of the intellect' with 'optimism of the will'. The problem with those who refuse to accept fully the death of social democracy, while failing to imagine radical alternatives to it, is that they do not demonstrate enough of either. To do so must mean refusing to accept that there is no alternative to neo-liberalism, while openly admitting that the current situation for the left is so drastic that we do not yet know exactly what the alternative might be. In fact, this is precisely the position shared by the participants in the global campaign for an alternative globalisation (as the newly fashionable French term *altermondialisation* has it). Openly unsure as to where we are going, we at least know that it cannot be back to social democracy, or even forward to social democracy Mark II or III. The only alternative is to accept fully that, as commentators like Mulgan have always insisted, party politics today cannot be genuinely participative - and so to look for a non-party politics that can be. The only alternative is to accept, as New Labour does, that existing forms of representative democracy must inevitably produce governments which implement neo-liberal agendas - and so to look to the invention of other kinds of democracy altogether. The only alternative is to accept, as Blair insists, that the nation state can never again do for its people what it did in the twentieth century - and so look for a radicalism which is truly international in scope. Of course this movement is in its infancy. Of course the social forums - congregations of activists, organisations, parties and people meeting on a global, continental, national, regional, or local scale - do not look now like the basis for some new, post-parliamentary democracy.[6] Of course they are full of cranks and fanatics. But the first meetings of the Chartists or the Workers' International must have looked much the same, and it is with an eye to the next hundred years and not only the next general election that this movement is trying to start to imagine a better world. What is most ironic about the relative indifference to this movement displayed in the pages of *Soundings* is that the politics exhibited here - from the Zapatista insurgency of Chiapas to the European Social Forum - is informed by precisely the kind of analysis made by the New Times analysis. Hall seems to wonder what would have happened if the analysis of Thatcherism had been made in a more adequately global context. Here, to an extent, is his answer: contemporary 'anti-capitalism' *is* internationalist New Times politics. It may look clumsy, naive and utopian, but it's this or New Labour. There is no Third Way.

This does not imply, by any means, that parliamentary politics is now irrelevant. There is a great deal to play for in the space between what New Labour would like to do now and what it can be forced to put off indefinitely by popular resistance and organised parliamentary opposition (the full marketisation of English Higher Education may yet fall into the latter category). But let there be no mistake: it is popular resistance and not social democratic hand-wringing which will make such outcomes possible. The task of figuring out just how to use 'state' institutions in the service of progressive ends is still one which cannot be deferred to some post-revolutionary future, and here the important work of policy-oriented think tanks like Catalyst remains essential. However, in this new context, all such proposals will prove ultimately sterile if they are not subtended by a recognition of the extent and intensity of neo-liberalism's opposition to reforms which thirty years ago would have been considered moderately social-democratic. The marshy middle ground between neo-liberalism and anti-capitalism, on which the 'soft left' once stood so confidently, has completely collapsed. But the idea that this renders meaningless the distinction between left and right is one which would only make sense to

---

6. See www.worldsocialforum.org www.fes-esf.org www.londonsocialforum.org

those who have fallen through the hole and find themselves groping blindly in the dark. In truth, this situation leaves an unbridgeable gap between those with any desire at all to pursue egalitarian political objectives and the agents of US-led capitalism. This may leave a role for something resembling twentieth-century social democracy, but it would have to be so far removed from its antecedents as to be virtually unrecognisable. In particular, any such project will only have credibility with a wider public if it publicly acknowledges what most people already know: that to pursue even mildly egalitarian reforms will place any government in direct confrontation with the forces of neo-liberalism. This is why the latest statement from a dissatisfied group of Labour MPs is so very interesting. The 'New Wave Labour' group, is calling for the government to engage in radical democratic experiments, and explicitly refers to Porto Alegre, the Brazilian home of the World Social Forum, famous for its participatory city budget-making process.[7] It is fantastically heartening to hear Labour MPs talking in these terms. The trouble is, for Labour to have its Porto Alegre, it would have to become something like the Brazilian Workers' Party: more a mass social movement than a European-style professional party. There seems very little chance of such an outcome. More realistically, MPs like these might hope to become part of some wider, looser coalition of forces, but it would have to be a coalition all of whose members were prepared - like the Workers' Party government in Brazil - to tell the public the truth about their place in a global struggle.

The logical conclusion of this observation is for those fifteen MPs and all those who support them to accept that there is absolutely no chance of persuading the New Labour leadership to change direction, because the New Labour leadership is utterly convinced that the terms in which the group frames its demands are historically redundant. In the medium term, only outright opposition to the Labour leadership and its commitment to neo-liberal modernisation can be the logical conclusion of those demands. However, those demands can themselves only become meaningful if they develop into a mature critique of the whole current

---

7. See Angela Eagle MP *A Deeper Democracy*, Catalyst 2003; www.catalystforum.org.uk; www.newwavelabour.co.uk

apparatus of representative democracy, and an acknowledgement that any attempt to implement experiments in radical democracy, like that in Porto Alegre, must put its practitioners into direct opposition to global capital and explicitly in league with the forces of anti-capitalism the world over.

So what is to be done? To paraphrase Hall and Finlayson et al, and to add my own gloss: we are faced with a government committed to the implementation of a neo-liberal project - forced, like Thatcherism, pragmatically to make concessions to a range of social constituencies along the way, but even more deeply committed than Thatcherism to the ideology of competitive individualism at the level of cultural and social politics. We are also faced with a labour movement apparently determined to keep mistaking those pragmatic concessions for signs that the government is about to change course permanently; and one that is largely indifferent to the global anti-corporate movement which is trying to carry out the necessary work of re-imagining democracy for the twenty-first century. In this context, the respectable left still seems unable to accept the death of social democracy. Unwilling to mourn it properly and move on, it persists in a kind of melancholic mania, of which the latest glut of neo-social democratic manifestos is a symptom, positing as they all do the utterly utopian vision of a revival of social democracy by means of those very institutions (the World Trade Organisation, the European Union, etc) which have been brought into being to destroy it, without ever addressing the strategic question of how to organise countervailing forces to those which would clearly oppose their vision every inch of the way.[8] The task for those of us who accept this analysis is clear. We must work to exorcise this spectre, to persuade those sections of the labour movement - from trade union branches to the Parliamentary Labour Party - who remain complicit with New Labour and hope to persuade it to change course that they are wasting their time, and to build bridges between them and the global struggle against neo-liberalism. We must work to assist that movement in the task of creating a postmodern socialism.

Strategically, this will be a matter of persuading many of those constituencies who still see in New Labour the only alternative to a return to Tory rule to stop

8. See Eagle's paper; see also www.compassonline.org.uk; Lent et al, *Progressive Globalisation: Towards international social democracy*, Fabian Society 2003, etc.

shoring up this neo-liberal regime without abandoning the field of political struggle altogether. This is where we see that Hall's characterisation of New Labour as a mixed project is absolutely right at the crucial *strategic* level of analysis; for what continues to distinguish New Labour from Thatcherism is that it is strategically dependent on the support of constituencies to its left. This is the potential weakness which any future progressive project must seek to exploit, dis-articulating the New Labour coalition and re-articulating its more radical elements with those constituencies excluded from it altogether. The government is supported by a bloc which includes many elements - from constituency Labour activists to trade-union leaders - without whom no alternative can succeed. Any effective opposition to neo-liberal hegemony must begin the work of disaggregating this block and forming new coalitions.

Finally, an example of the price to be paid if such new coalitions do not emerge. In the UK, the trade union leaderships could already have led a successful popular campaign against the PFI and the privatisation of education services if they had bothered to try. This is a policy so detested, even in the heart of Middle England, that the government has had to rely on the collusion of the press in failing to report its operation and effects, knowing that it would never win a political argument over the issue. On a local level, as in Newcastle, there have been successful campaigns against privatisations. No doubt more typical, however, is the experience of the campaign against the privatisation of education services where I live in Waltham Forest, which collapsed amidst a general sense that this was a struggle which could only be fought at a national level, with the support of the trade union leaderships. Instead, the unions have been putting their energy into producing detailed critiques of this policy which no-one supported in the first place; hoping, it seems, to dissuade the government from pursuing it. Such hopes have proved utterly barren, and a historic opportunity for a truly popular campaign against neo-liberalism may already have been lost.

Of course, to have really launched such a campaign would have been to cross a Rubicon from which, thus far, almost all of the union leaderships have shied away. For to launch a popular, broad-based campaign against a government policy not only on grounds of its direct effects on their members' work and conditions, but on a point of political principle, and to do so outside the confines of the Labour Party conference, would be to acknowledge, finally, that the century which began with the formation of the Labour Representation Committee in February 1900 is over. It would be to acknowledge that the unions - the only organisations on the left with the resources to do so - must take a lead against this programme of marketisation, finding a new political voice in a world in which they can never again expect the Labour Party to be that for them. The Labour Party and its membership may yet have a positive role to play, but being the exclusive political voice of the trade unions is not it. They and we should take a lead from Newcastle and from Porto Alegre. We must finally accept that it is no use carping on the 'mistakes' being made by a government which shares none of our values. The only effective criticism will be one which works actively to demonstrate that, contrary to New Labour's own deeply-held conviction, another world is possible.

Thinking the global locally

Roundtable discussion with Katharine Ainger, Jane Foot, Clare Joy *and* Doreen Massey

In the lead up to the European Social Forum which will take place in London in autumn 2004, Soundings *asks how we might organise politically to take account of the global influences on local places and the influence of the local on the global. This question goes to the heart of creating new forms of radical politics that can meet the challenge of a globalising world. The discussion was chaired by* Jonathan Rutherford, *a member of the* Soundings *editorial group.*

Doreen The big question is how do we think about the relationship between the local and the global. We need to create a politics that is both local and global. I think that on both left and right there is a tendency to think of globalisation as being somehow 'up there' or 'out there'. The local and 'place' get posed as where real people actually live, and the global becomes something abstract. I think this is untenable. We have a fairly good understanding in the academic left world and in political struggles of the global construction of the local. That's important. But we don't think about the local construction of the global. We tend to think of the local as victim - there is no way that the Square Mile is a victim of globalisation.

Katharine There is a reason that people make these global powers into abstractions and talk about them in a virtual sense. Where does the money circulating the globe exist? You can't touch the web of networks and relationships that make up the financial markets. How do we track their very real connections and the real people making the decisions? There is also a problem in polarising local places between those subjected to globalisation and those who dole it out.

There are immigrant workers in the Square Mile, the cleaners and so on. It's not possible to divide up the physical geography so simply.

Doreen I would agree on your second point. But all 'global flows' touch the ground somewhere, and sometimes - as in the case of the City of London - their locations are very important to them. Every place is a mixture of dominant and subordinate relations.

Clare I've got two hats I would wear here. First, I'm a policy thinker with the WDM, whose mandate is to look at how local activists in the UK challenge global processes. In the UK, we're behind a lot of the European political activists when it comes to meaningfully articulating global processes in local activism and local campaigns. We've seen in Europe the rise of the ATTAC movement. No way would that develop here. Why not is an important question.

My second hat is my involvement in local food regeneration community programmes. In a very local way corporations and communities are challenging each other in the context of food. This has a very practical dimension. How do global processes impact locally, and how do communities challenge them?

Doreen Why do you think ATTAC could never take off in the UK?

Clare When people think about global activism in the UK, they think about the work of Christian Aid, Action Aid. The development charities here have a big profile as campaigners on global issues - perhaps more so than in other European countries. They've got much bigger public profiles. Also, the role unions have played has been very important. The unions here don't have the same tradition of involvement in larger political spaces like the European unions have in ATTAC in France and Austria.

Jane My interest is the future of local government, and the mobilisation of community as a way of transforming local government. I'm interested in how we build a network of organisations, activists and people who are engaged in different ways at a local level - something that connects to and understands the global context, rather than having just the traditional narrow, community focus on services, however important that is. In the kind of organisations I work with there are very few people involved who are also global activists. The WDM local group, for example, is not likely to be on the list to be consulted about the future of public services. It's in a different world.

There is currently a whole set of policies and initiatives which are giving local government responsibility for creating a sense of place. I'm interested in a practical politics that not only connects global activists to the local, but connects local activists to the global.

Katharine I think the left in the UK is afraid of a discussion around place because it is so dominated by the right - as, for example, the countryside alliance. In France activities around locality are how ordinary people are getting involved in progressive global politics.

Doreen I think one way that place became important in the UK was all the factory closures in the 1980s, and then the development of the branch plant economy phenomenon. People saw their regions, particularly in the North, Scotland and Wales, being dominated by multi-national corporations. Low paid labour and the fly-by-night factory brought a consciousness of being locked into a global economy. I think this helped to generate a rather conservative localism - our own capitalists are better than nasty foreign capitalists.

Jane That kind of local protectionism is very contradictory. For instance, a council in Cornwall that publishes a booklet listing local sources of food sees it as an issue of sustainability, protecting the local economy, and promoting a Cornish identity. For them it's a progressive identity thing.

Doreen Katharine, were you thinking about José Bové?

Katharine Yes - or at least his union the *Confederation Paysannes*. They held a summer festival to celebrate thirty years of the radical farmers' occupation of the Larzac Plateau. 350,000 people turned up. Breton fishermen's unions with their fish stalls, Arab migrants from the Paris *Banlieues*, families driving down in trucks - a complete cross-section of French society, with radical workshops and free music. It was a broad-based social movement. It's hard to imagine this happening in the UK. But it's my vision of what the ideal social forum should look like

Doreen I think José Bové has tried to make it an open and non-defensive movement. To value the Roquefort cheese and the Breton fish, but not to make this a nationalistic or simply anti-American issue, but rather one against the multinational homogenisation of food.

Katharine I think one of the ways José Bové has managed this is by being part of *La Vie Campesina*, the international peasant farmers' union. *La Vie Campesina* is an extraordinary phenomenon, which includes enormous peasant movements in Brazil, Indonesia and India. Scottish crofters and farm groups in the US are also part of it. They're asking how people who are set against one another in the global market place can get together to fight the global powers. And, especially, how do you do this when you're rooted to the place where you grow your food. Farmers can't get up and move their farm. *Vie Campesina* is one of the most interesting examples of a politics that is very local but is operating globally at the same time. They've been at the forefront of the globalisation movement from the beginning.

Doreen They have a global politics that manages to recognise all the differences between the constituent movements as well as having a linked politics. Do you work with them Clare?

Clare We do. What's interesting about them is that they identify as a local-global movement.

Jane How would local activists here connect to that politics? What's the equivalent in the UK? Food production here involves a tiny proportion of the population. Most of the politics are pretty regressive. Our relationship with it here is mostly as consumers of food. It's a very different kind of politics, and one which is not necessarily organised around place.

Jonathan Are subsistence farming communities and producers more linked with a local place than city dwellers? It's interesting that it is these people, rather than those living in global cosmopolitan cities, who have created a global/local politics.

Doreen I'm wary about that notion of a relationship to the soil. It's not an unquestionable rootedness. There are also the indigenous movements who are making their own global networks, and international trade unions are grappling with some of these issues.

Katharine What frightens me is the isolation and alienation where there has been a breakdown in a sense of place. The vacuum is filled by a nationalistic, anti-migrant, racist discourse, which is a way to recreate identity and connection through a mythologising of roots or place. So we get afraid of talking about place at all, because we don't want to add fuel to nationalism and racism.

Doreen We have to rethink it. For example, I think there is a certain conception of London as being multi-ethnic. There is an enormous pride in its diversity. Keeping in mind the existing racism, nevertheless there is a self perception around which is about difference.

Jane There is a sense that the local is disempowering and full of uncertainty. One has to defend it in order to feel secure in it. People think, 'global troubles are visited on my local patch and I can't do anything about them. I just have to live with the consequences.' And the idea of place becomes fixed and nostalgic - it used to be like this and now it's not. It's been taken over.

The government has responded to this reaction by promoting a discourse of community in which there is no conflict, and which suggests that everybody shares the same views about what a place means and what its future is. It ends up trying to fix an idea of community, draw lines around it, rather than talking about difference, or having a definition of place that contains difference, or is connected globally as opposed to being turned inward.

Jonathan The right has played on this desire for security. However the left' s got a much bigger problem if it wants to be open to difference and the global, or at least to get people to recognise the influence of the global. How do you get people to feel open to it and also secure in it?

Jane You need a sense of place from which you can feel you can affect your quality of life. That's the bit that's missing. The local feels like it's being visited on. It's the victim and not the place of power.

Clare I think we've tried to deal with this problem by focusing on specific contexts. The specific feels tangible, there's something you can do about it. But the difficulty is that the political strategies we're developing around globalisation then come from specifics rather than from the general political context and the ideas and ideologies which surround it. This takes us back a decade to when there was a critique of the anti-globalisation movement in terms of its being a single issue campaign.

Doreen What people get agitated about is the disintegration of their lives, and that gets picked up in certain particular things; maybe food, maybe privatisation, maybe the closure of the post office. The issues are important. Globalisation is a massive, complex constellation of single issues. Single issue campaigns have been a positive strength of the counter globalisation movement. Getting in there at the level of things which have geographies that you can collar is absolutely brilliant.

Clare Doreen, you and Katharine have been involved in the social forums. For many of us this has been a challenging experience. In Europe, for example, the European Social Forum (ESF) is yet to articulate change in the context of the specific issues that groups, local communities and regional activists have been working on. The social forum movement has a mandate to bring together the myriad of local activity that is challenging corporate globalisation, but there's a lot of work to do if they are going to achieve this and not get stuck in trying to articulate the big idea.

Jonathan Can you be more specific?

Clare The organisation of the last ESF gathering in Paris in November 2003 was in danger of being dominated by political parties. In the UK it has been the SWP. This was very clear in the way the agenda was set up and the discussions were moved forward. For example there was no real space for discussion about common local progressive agriculture in Europe. It just didn't exist. The organisation of the social forum has to keep up with people who are engaging in local alternatives around a specific issue and also creating Europe wide networks.

Doreen That's crazy. The forum is supposed to be precisely that kind of space.

Clare It's got a long way to go to fulfil its mandate.

Jonathan What were the discussions in Paris?

Clare It was a three day conference with some very eminent European speakers. But if we think about how we connect people across Europe who are working in local areas and trying to change things in small ways, sitting down in front of a panel of eleven speakers and listening is not a very effective method. The discussions were generally abstract. They weren't rooted in campaigning experience.

Katharine It's a shame, because a lot of people in the movement have been looking at reinventing forms of democracy. The heart of the globalisation movement is a democracy movement. It's about getting people's voices heard; not just the intellectuals. Social movements are so frustrated at not being able to get into the main event that they are beginning to organise their own parallel forums. But social forums must be places of genuine dialogue and democracy, open to all, if they are to work. The politics of parties is to see people as potential recruits to help get them into power. They don't see people as having equal dialogue with them. I don't think they're interested in democracy. And that's my fear of what will happen when the European Social Forum comes to the UK this autumn.

Jane Democracy is probably the biggest shared political issue between us - which we grapple with in local and global communities: forms of democracy that engage people in dialogue and that are going to be effective. We need to devise forms of democracy which can take us from the local to the global.

Local electoral democracy has been completed drained of content. The attempt to create participative democracy locally is fraught with difficulties. It's often confined to a very small segment of people who are already active in a traditional set of organisations, with very traditional ways of seeing things. In the end all the consultation processes are framed in the managerialism that dominates local government. They don't fundamentally challenge the assumptions on which policy decisions are made.

Doreen The same thing is happening to regional governments. New Labour says they mustn't be talking shops. But talking shops are really important. A lot of where politics happens is in having conflicts around what is going to be the politics of this place. We need to think how we organise new forms of democracy. We live in a world where most democracies are territorially organised. It's a huge challenge to construct a public in a world which consists of relationships that are global, and where every decision we make has repercussions miles away.

I think this attempt to globalise local democratic forms is what Porte Alegre has been trying to think about. The *Confederation Paysanne* is an example of trying to think of the global through relations, flows and connections rather than territories. It's a conceptual step forward.

Clare It's beginning to happen in anti-corporate activism. For example, a campaign against Onyx Waste in Brighton hooks up with activists in Delhi where the same company is operating.

Jane We've got more idea about how to create those kinds of global networks than how to link people campaigning on different issues in the same area - for instance, those campaigning around waste in Brighton with people at the other end of town who are campaigning against the closure of a residential home. The anti-corporate networks have a shared enemy. But in the local context, the conflicts of priorities are between local groups and interests. There has to be a democratic process which allows debate. It's very difficult to think about a politics which doesn't have a territorial base.

Doreen I tend to feel more like Clare. But I agree that it is difficult to link an anti-Onyx struggle around waste with a housing issue down the road.

Katharine Ideally there would be a Brighton social forum which would help create these links. We need more of them in the UK. I find the London social forum encouraging. I'd given up on political spaces being kept open without being colonised by particular groups in the UK, but this one has been kept open.

Jonathan What is the relationship of social forums to the formal structures of local government and party political power? There seem to be few possibilities of the Labour Party being open to these new kinds of politics.

Katharine The attempt from the top down in the Labour Party to engage in the language of devolution and local participation has killed it stone dead. The government got excited about citizen juries but as soon as the citizens got critical of the government they dropped the idea. They started using marketing-style focus groups instead. I would argue for the power of sheer critical mass from the ground up. Building our own legitimacy is our source of power. I think any attempt to become part of the governing structures will see the shutting down of the democratic spaces.

Jane The last attempt by government was the national debate about GM, which I don't suppose they will repeat. People came up with the wrong answer.

Clare Even though it was so controlled and undemocratic.

Doreen I see the Labour Party as on another planet. Critical mass is a good term.

Jonathan Do you see this critical mass coming to bear on the Labour Party structures in order for the Labour Party to carry out the changes that you want, or do you go into representative democracy yourself? How do you practically, pragmatically and ideologically create a politics that can get to grips with power?

Jane I think the social forum model is where it's at, because people will come to social forums with these conflicting perspectives and interests. They are places of dialogue which create something for people to organise around. If you take it into the party you lose that dialogue. Social spaces for critical dialogue are what is missing.

Doreen The editorial in *Soundings* issue 1 recognised politics as being about more than what happens in Westminster. What about feminism, parts of the green movement? Social movements have radical effects.

Katharine The idea that one must get into power and then implement change isn't working. Enormous compromises are made. I don't think we should ignore the conventional realm of party politics, but we should see it as a defensive strategy. Yes, vote for Lula in Brazil, but don't imagine that you've won when he gets elected. There's a whole global structure out there that's preventing him bringing in the kind of changes we need. We do need a parallel process - a politics from below.

Doreen It's about trying to change the climate of opinion, so that it enables Lula to win power and not then think that that is the end of it.

Jonathan In this analysis one tends to remain in an oppositional role on the outside. In a sense we don't sully our hands with the messy business of power and responsibility. Who is going to do that? The Labour Party appears to have abandoned social democracy. How do we create not only spaces to think about the kind of lives that we are living, but organisations which engage with the structures of the state - getting a lever on policy decisions, getting hold of real resources?

Katharine There isn't an easy answer. As mainstream politics is losing its legitimacy in the eyes of a lot of people, it's possible to do parallel building of our own legitimacy. When you do that, you do see resources moving to communities. I don't think oppositional politics is a good description of this. One can make a positive agenda. We're building something.

Clare We've been looking at that building process. If we want to build global networks, we have to create local social forums in the UK. I don't like the term capacity building, but we've got an awful lot of political capacity building to do.

That's when you begin to notice a critical mass, it's empowering. Our involvement with party politics should be to challenge and check it.

Doreen It isn't about just being oppositional. Our understanding of globalisation has been transformed, from seeing it as a technical, inevitable necessity that was just a force of nature into a recognition that there are different forms of globalisation and they are not necessary. Labour has taken the politics out of economics. The globalisation movement has put it back. We've not come up with an answer to what other kinds of globalisation we might want, but it's an important achievement.

Jane I think politicising issues and processes that have been presented as technical is one of the most important developments. Joining the Labour Party is not where this happens. Politicisation happens in other spaces like international networks.

Jonathan The question I'm concerned with is, what do you do about the formal structures of political power?

Jane Yes. What do you do when, for example, the local council wants to close down a library? Politicising economics or globalisation may or may not help you.

Katharine There was a lot of publicity about the people of Cochabamba in Bolivia and their successful protest against the privatisation of the water. But you never hear about what happened afterwards. The Council which ran it was divided up between members of the public who'd been part of the Coordinadoran - who'd overturned the water company - members of trade unions, members of local government. It was a model of participatory management, but it's been very problematic.

Doreen The 1980s left urban local governments did force you to get to grips with the practical details. We can't avoid this question of responsibility, and I don't think political parties aren't important. In Latin America, the elections that have happened, including Argentina, have created an important shift.

Clare This question of how we engage with formal structures of government is important for us in WDM. One of the biggest problems now for the water system in Cochabamba is that they can't get finance for investment. On a global and a local level we need to think about how we get to grips with these issues.

Katharine We do have to start talking about the details, but then again a lot of practical solutions already exist. For example you could get finance for local investment by selling your own bonds; it's not easy, but there are possibilities for economic democracy.

Jonathan I think it's very difficult when New Labour has shifted agency toward market solutions and managerial styles. They have shut down political resources, the role models if you like, for doing this kind of politics.

Jane Ironically, the government has created a certain amount of opportunity for participation which is not dominated by party politics. They have gone down the road of having multi-stakeholder boards, and involving local groups in things like foundation hospitals. Very often, however, they are filled with individuals who have no infrastructure by which they can represent the local perspective or connect back to any kind of local community.

Jonathan It encourages a quite individual relationship to the state apparatus. Would one want an ideology to start emerging for example, in the social forums, which would provide a perspective of the world people could draw on as a resource?

Jane Certainly, we need to develop some kind of small 'p' politics at a local level about what are the priorities and values.

Katharine It's a methodology, rather than an ideology. It's about the process.

Doreen I think social forums are for debates. They don't take positions. I do think we need to have a debate about what we do with the global institutions like the World Bank, whose projects and development financing are determined by neo-liberal criteria and the influence of multi-national companies. We can't simply call for the abolition of the WTO. There's a huge lack of democracy within it, and a huge imbalance in negotiating power. It's run as if it is dealing with technical matters, when in fact they are highly political. But we cannot do without global institutions. We have to work out what to do about the global levels of government.

Clare In the run up to the European Social Forum in London we should also be supporting and working with the local social forums in the UK - London, Manchester, Newcastle. We must ensure that the European Social Forum complements, rather than exhausts, the small local processes.

Katharine We need to build these local forums across the country in order to create a broad based democratic momentum which will lead up to the European Social Forum, and perhaps transform it into the kind of space we always imagined it could be.

Shuffling back to equality?

Ruth Levitas

Ruth Levitas *argues that the Compass manifesto does not make a serious enough challenge to New Labour. Its too-ready acceptance of the market, its underlying meritocratic assumptions, and its weak defence of equality, show that the Compass group have not wholly succeeded in breaking free of New Labour doublethink.*

In September 2003, representatives of Labour's most influential think-tanks, including Demos, Catalyst, the IPPR and the Fabian Society, joined forces with a handful of prominent academics to issue a statement intended as the basis of a new pressure group, Compass. This manifesto was publicised - sometimes in articles by its signatories - as an attempt to reinstate egalitarianism as a core principle of New Labour's project. However, in my view it provides only a slight and equivocal defence of equality. This article considers whether this equivocation results, as Stuart Hall suggests, from the character of New Labour itself, and confusion on the part of its supporters; and it argues that a stronger version of equality is needed to challenge neo-liberalism in both the short and the long term.

The Compass document is important because its signatories occupy strategic positions for influencing public discourse and political policy. (One name notable for its absence from the manifesto, though, is that of the ex-Director of the IPPR Matthew Taylor, known to have played a role in its drafting. Taylor has been made responsible for drafting Labour's actual manifesto for the next election.) And it is important because it seeks to give a more redistributive and social democratic direction to the Labour government. Compass is proclaimed as a vision for the democratic left - even if its cover statement reads like an excerpt from the new Clause IV:

> Our central claim is that the richness of human potential in today's society requires both pluralism and egalitarianism to be embraced and combined in radical, distinctive ways by democratic left politics. If each person has equal worth, the limitations on their achievement and contribution must be systematically broken down. This requires public action and investment. But the uniqueness of this potential makes social diversity, openness and freedom equally important. The major implication of this position is that capitalism should be directed in ways that align it with human need, rather than managed as an unstoppable force.

The core argument of the Compass document is that 'the primacy of political and democratic values over those of the market must be at the heart of any Labour renewal'.

In contrast to such hopes, Stuart Hall reads New Labour as a new hybrid between neo-liberalism and social democracy, linked in a transformist mode in which the social democratic element is systematically suborned and redirected to neo-liberal ends (*Soundings* 24). A project that sets out to reverse this relation is doomed, because it is based on a fundamental misunderstanding of the nature of New Labour, which governs in the interests of capital, while engaged in limited redistribution by stealth to keep its traditional supporters on board. This 'double shuffle'- governing in the interests of one constituency, while sustaining electoral support in another - is sustained by 'spin'. Ambiguous rhetoric is essential to disguising underlying conflicts of interest that are always resolved in favour of neo-liberalism. Spin is therefore intrinsic to the project, rather than an unfortunate and dispensable addition. Hall suggests that the concepts that are used to perform the double shuffle confuse even those close to New Labour, misleading social democrats into hoping that they can influence the project in a less neo-liberal direction.

It is not hard to find examples of this double shuffle. The changes made to the concept of social exclusion are illustrative here. This concept used to be part of a primarily redistributive discourse about poverty and inequality, but New Labour (with a little help from the European Union) has embedded the notion of social exclusion in a variable mixture of a social integrationist discourse focused on paid work, and a moral underclass discourse focused on social and cultural conformity. In the first months of Blair's government, it was evident that this multiplicity of meanings was part of the point: it facilitated the acceptance by neo-liberals of redistributive policies under the guise of fostering social cohesion, or - more often - the acceptance by social democrats of potentially punitive and always constraining policies, in the name of a limited redistribution. Even when 'poverty' returned to the New Labour lexicon, the line between the deserving and the undeserving poor was redrawn on the basis of working age: *child* poverty and *pensioner* poverty became legitimate causes of concern, but not poverty itself. The causes of poverty continue to be represented as supply-side failures of 'employability' and cultural failure such as 'poverty of aspirations', while the annual audit purporting to address poverty and social exclusion is called *Opportunity For All*.

The 'third way' is a similarly flexible concept, initially supported by at least some of the Compass signatories - who were, as they say, 'enthusiasts for the original New Labour project'. Compass now redeploys the spatial metaphor, arguing that 'New Labour stands at a crossroads'; 'The Government appears to have lost its way'; and 'If New Labour is lost, it needs help to find its way'. But the third way was always contested, as was evident in the e-mail debate organised by the virtual think-tank Nexus in 1998, to which several of the current group contributed. As Gavin Kelly and Andrew Gamble argued then, there were at least three alternative meanings: a middle way between two viable (or indeed unviable) alternatives such as capitalism and socialism/ old left and new right; the creation of a new alignment, the so-called 'radical centre', 'beyond left and right'; or a revival of social democracy offering a clear alternative to neo-liberalism. Stuart White argued that the divisions in the terrain occupied by the third way could be identified as being between egalitarians and meritocrats, and between liberals and communitarians, and that this internal pluralism was both a weakness and a strength: 'It is a weakness in so far as it implies that appeals to "the third way" in political argument are likely to remain ambiguous … It is a strength insofar as it provides the kind of elasticity necessary for building a broad-based political coalition stretching across the political spectrum to marginalize the free-market Right - such being Tony Blair's more or less stated ambition'.

This statement was clearly an attempt to redefine rather than to describe the New Labour project, for White went on to say that it was essential to contest the more conservative, less social democratic interpretations. Nevertheless, there is an element of confusion here, since it was abundantly clear even in 1997 that for the architects of New Labour the third way was not about a revived social democracy as an alternative to neo-liberalism. Blair might argue that New Labour 'stands firmly in the social-democratic tradition', but it was 'with a new hard edge to its economic thinking'; and in so far as New Labour criticised the new right, these criticisms had 'nothing to do with living in a market economy'.

In locating the third way as being between or beyond 'Old Left and New Right', much hinged on the meaning of 'Old Left'. If the first and second ways were socialism and laissez-faire capitalism, then social democracy and a mixed economy themselves constituted a third way. But New Labour placed the third way as being between that 'centrist' social democratic position and the 'free' market; this was essentially to locate it as a centre right position, with everyone from Roy Hattersley leftwards included in the old left. The continuities with Thatcherism were evident. The New Right involved a synthesis of free market and strong state, whereas New Labour's third way could be seen as a 'soft' synthesis of market forces and 'community', where the role of 'community' is (actually) to mop up the damage done by market forces and mediate the policing functions of the state, and (discursively) to serve as legitimation of this. David Marquand argued that the role of third way rhetoric was to 'de-legitimise all pre-Blair social-democratic thought, by lumping it together with clause four state socialism and even, God help us, "really existing" Communist bloc socialism'; to 'fortify neo-liberal hegemony', marginalising its critics by defining them as out-of-date; to falsify the history of the centre-left; to misrepresent the nature of global capitalism; and to feed dangerous forms of populism. Marquand was clear that it was not the right but the left that were marginalised by the flexible concept of the third way. He warned against the hubris of attempting to reclaim the term for social democracy: 'Your nice little tin whistle will be drowned out by the drums of the real inventors of the language, who are using it quite deliberately … as a way of marginalising all actual or potential critics of centralist populism'.

This revisiting of the Nexus debate suggests that at least some of the Compass signatories were not deluded about the nature of New Labour; and this earlier clarity sits oddly with the woolliness of the new manifesto. Staying with Labour as it marches rightwards may result from blind loyalty, or it could stem from an unwillingness to cede the Party to its hijackers; or it may rest on the old claim that even right-wing Labour governments are more susceptible to pressure from the left, precisely because they have to keep their traditional constituency on board (though the lesson of the Blair governments is surely the opposite: that New Labour is *more* effectively neo-liberal than Thatcherism, because it leaves no organisational basis for resistance). Or it may simply be that there is nowhere else to go.

The Compass project demands a change in political direction, and it is rightly ambitious. It calls for a 'vision of the world we want and the values that should inform it', and insists that 'our vision must … be more than just managing the current system better', and must seek to 'transform it'. This vision includes social democratic renewal, a re-invigoration of left of centre politics, progressive values, pluralism and egalitarianism. We can ignore the rhetorical appeal to 'progressive values' and left-of-centre politics. Words like new, modern, and progressive imply 'good' but are devoid of content, while 'left-of-centre' recycles all the problems of the third way. A key issue, however, is how Compass constructs the relationship between the market and 'social democracy', and how it attempts the reinstatement of egalitarianism as a core value for the democratic left; and because of the failure to challenge the neo-liberal core of New Labour, these terms are discursively constructed in ways that pose very little challenge to current policy directions. Whatever the mix of hope, confusion, and desperation inspiring Compass, its treatment of social democracy and equality demonstrates precisely the transformism Hall identifies. The different uses of the term 'equality' can be seen as part of the double shuffle described by Hall. Being trapped between the knowledge that radical change is necessary, and the sense that very little is possible, produces at least the appearance of confusion - and makes the very changes Compass seeks less possible. If equality is to be put back on the political agenda, it will need a much more trenchant defence than this, and a much more fundamental break with neo-liberalism.

Renewing social democracy

Social democracy in Britain has historically involved support for a mixed economy; commitment to a strong public sphere in which democratic values and processes take precedence over the market; and commitment to (varying degrees of) redistribution both through the tax and benefit systems and through the funding of public services. Such broad principles can in themselves gloss over quite significant political differences, while a 'revived' social democracy suggests further variations. Compass identifies the current crisis of New Labour as a failure to mobilise broad support behind a 'popular, successful, social democratic renewal', but is very unclear about what social democracy is. That modern social democracy 'values individual rights through community action, allowing members of the public to play an active and constructive role in real decisions that affect their lives' tells us very little. The document asserts the importance of the public sphere, public services and redistribution. Yet the issue of the limits of markets - a crucial point in differentiating social democracy from neo-liberalism - is barely addressed. For Compass, social democracy clearly does not involve a mixed economy. Public ownership is dismissed, despite the appalling consequences of rail privatisation and the consequent subsidy of the private sector out of public funds: 'In rewriting Clause 4 [New Labour] rightly redefined community, not public ownership, as the mechanism for citizens to realise their true potential'. Three separate statements relating social democracy and the market unpack into conflicting positions. First: 'Social democrats have always held that markets need to be used, not suppressed'. This is not true, since the so-called social-democratic consensus of the post-war era embraced the principle of a mixed economy, presuming that there were areas of collective provision where markets should indeed be suppressed, and indeed excluded. Second: 'Social democrats always insisted that markets were to serve people, not vice versa'. This is tendentious, collapsing the quite different claims that markets *do* serve people, that they *should* serve people and that they *can* serve people. Third: 'Decisions need to be made through the democratic process, not just the market one'. This does at least suggest a potential tension between the market and the public sphere, although the 'both-and' formulation does not clearly give democratic *decisions* priority over market *outcomes*.

'Both-and' is one of New Labour's central discursive strategies, found in such dyads as 'economic efficiency and social justice' - a declaration of compatibility by sentence construction, evading inherent contradictions, especially since economic efficiency is a code for increasing marketisation. Compass contains similar formulations. That capitalism 'should be directed in ways that align it with human need' excludes the possibility that these two are in fact antagonistic. To state that, 'In a good society, global capitalism is managed for the

> 'if equality is to be put back on the political agenda it will need a much more trenchant defence than this'

benefit of the least well off, not the richest' does not confront the possibility that global capitalism cannot be managed for the poorest, and is (therefore) incompatible with a good society. Such oppositions and difficulties have to be argued through; they cannot be annihilated by assertion. There is some suggestion at the very end of the document that environmental considerations may constitute a potential challenge to capitalism. To argue that 'New Labour has failed to strike creative compromises with capitalism on terms which protect the environment and society' is to acknowledge at least a degree of conflict, as is the assertion of 'the need for regulation to manage capitalism for the benefit of the many and the future of the planet'. Consequently: 'Global capitalism needs more management, not less' (although, at the same time, 'Government must learn to govern less'). There is no suggestion in all this that the value they ostensibly place on the public sphere and on collective provision must place limits on markets. The concession to the market and its dominance is already made. Compass attempts to revive social democracy while abandoning key elements of its economic basis, much as the late Paul Hirst tried, in *Associative Democracy*, to resurrect the communal and democratic forms of guild socialism espoused by G. D. H. Cole, while rejecting the claims for collective ownership on which it was based.

A neo-liberal hegemony of possessive individualism intrudes even into Compass's discussion of the public sphere. Common social goods such as transport, communication infrastructure and public services, and investment in these, are held to be important. But the erosion of collective protection against risk is taken for granted, and the move to individual provision endorsed. Even the policy recommendation of redistributing wealth 'to where the difference it can make to well-being is greatest - to those with least', is about asset-based welfare: 'Capital assets - savings, shares and home ownership - should be brought within the reach of all citizens, so that wealth ownership and the benefits it brings can be spread throughout the community'. The aim is that: 'Everyone should have that safety margin that middle class people take for granted'. In other words, the spread of *individual* wealth ownership is supported because it provides *individual* protection against risk.

Compass comments on the fact that conflicts between neo-liberal and egalitarian principles have been systematically resolved in favour of the market. It argues that the challenge for New Labour was 'to find ways of egalitarian redistribution to coexist with the needs of enterprise', but that demands from the private sector for reduced taxation and deregulation have been met, while inequality remains excessively high. This argument that current inequalities are too high is about as far as the new egalitarianism goes however. The 'cornerstone of left politics' is presented not as 'equality', but 'reducing inequality'. There is also a typically Blairite endorsement of 'equal worth'. Equality of opportunity, not equality of condition, is supported - and that only weakly: 'a good society is one in which people's life chances become more equal as a result of social and economic institutions designed to benefit the least advantaged and most vulnerable'. Arguments against current levels of inequality are largely pragmatic. Excessive inequality undermines social cohesion, access to opportunity, and democracy: 'we cannot have equal democratic rights when the resources available to different groups and individuals are so unequal'. But if 'it is unjust for so many to remain in poverty while others live in fabulous wealth', there is no sense that inequality itself is unjust, or that there is a problem about the rich. It might be argued that establishing this limited critique begins to move the agenda gradually in the direction of greater equality. But the background assumption is that inequality is natural and acceptable, and is a problem only when it is extreme and generates poverty. Such arguments do not, in fact, reinstate egalitarianism at all, but rather accept, defend and naturalise inequality, while arguing that there is rather too much of it. Even the observation that 'huge inequalities remain and may be getting wider' implies that they are some kind of natural obstacle to be overcome, rather than the outcome of political decisions.

It is very easy to forget that current levels of inequality in the UK are relatively recent. Inequality was at its lowest in the late 1970s. But between 1979 and 1990, the reductions in income inequality of the previous century were wholly reversed. The Joseph Rowntree Foundation's 1995 *Inquiry Into Income and Wealth* attributed this to a mixture of economic restructuring, increasing dispersion in male earnings, and - crucially - changes in taxation and social security. In the UK, Corporation Tax fell from 52 to 33 per cent in 1997 to 30 per cent in 2001 (with the small companies rate dropping from 42 to 19 per cent). It now generates only 12 per cent of the total tax take, compared with 21 per cent in 1979. The top rate of income tax fell from 83 per cent in 1979 to 40 per cent: the rich saw their tax bills fall by amounts greater than the annual incomes of the poorest families. Income tax is now barely progressive beyond the lowest levels: the standard rate of income tax plus national insurance rolls in at 33 per cent; the top rate is just 41 per cent; and indirect taxation is heavily regressive. The share of total income going to the bottom ten per cent of people dropped from around 4 per cent in 1979 to around 2 per cent by 1990 - that is, one fifth of what they would have received under conditions of distributive equality. By 1990, the incomes of the poorest ten per cent, measured after housing costs are taken into account, were lower in real terms than in 1979. This was catastrophic. But the change in fortunes of the rich was even more dramatic. In 1979, the richest ten per cent received over twenty per cent of national income, or twice their share; by 1997 this had risen to twenty-eight per cent, and by 2002 to twenty-nine per cent, or nearly three times their share. In 1979, the top ten per cent had five times the share of the bottom group; by 2001/2, they had nearly fifteen times that share. These figures do not even begin to address the enormous differences in income associated with ethnicity, gender, age and region, nor inequalities in wealth and the ownership of different kinds of assets. Any substantial reduction in these inequalities would require measures as dramatic and controversial as those of the Thatcher years. This is not on the Compass agenda.

Table 1: *Percentage shares of total net income received by individuals in different deciles of the income distribution in 1979, 1990/1, 1996/7 and 2000/1, calculated after housing costs*

	1979	1990/1	1996/7	2001/2
Lowest 10%	4	2	2	2
Second 10%	6	4	4	4
Third 10%	7	5	5	5
Fourth 10%	7	7	6	7
Fifth 10%	8	7	8	7
Sixth 10%	10	10	9	9
Seventh 10%	11	10	10	10
Eighth 10%	12	12	13	12
Ninth 10%	14	16	15	15
Top 10%	21	27	28	29

Sources: 1979 & 1990/1, Joseph Rowntree Foundation Inquiry into Income and Wealth *(1995); 1996/7 and 2000/1,* Households Below Average Income 2003, *DWP*

The assumptions that are made about legitimate inequalities rest on a fundamental acceptance of market principles, and neo-liberal assumptions are so firmly entrenched that to challenge them involves apparently banal points. We currently distribute the social product not on the basis of effort, talent, social contribution or - least of all - need, but on the basis of the *price* people can exact for their labour. We think of *redistribution* as a post-hoc adjustment to these market outcomes. Compass's claim that the Blair government is the most redistributive on record clearly carries this sense - although even then it is not obviously true. But markets are not neutral distributive mechanisms. They are mechanisms that are embedded in social and legal structures that sanction and support the *redistribution* of the social product away from workers and towards capital. The major *distributive* changes effected under Thatcher were also *redistributive* in this sense. This process has intensified in recent decades: André Gorz argues that in the last quarter of the twentieth century there was a marked rise in the proportion of the global social product committed to dividends and executive salaries, and a concomitant fall in the proportion dedicated to wages, salaries and investment. The shift is the outcome of concessions made by nation states acting competitively to prevent the flight of capital - such as reductions in corporation tax.

Perhaps we should begin from somewhere else. A document calling for a vision of a good society needs to use a more utopian method, in the sense that it needs to define the principles of such a society *independently* of short-term politics, and without the assumption that a good society is, in fact, compatible with global (or any other kind of) capitalism. This calls for greater 'clarity about moral and ideological purpose and boldness about how it can be enacted' than Compass provides. But if you accept the initial principle, endorsed on more than one occasion by Blair, that people are of equal worth, then a much stronger defence of substantive equality, or equality of condition, follows.

Accroding to Compass, equality of worth implies the removal of 'limitations on [people's] achievement and contribution'. It implies, that is, equality of opportunity, not rights to a share - let alone an equal share - of the social product sufficient to their human flourishing. The implicit model here of a good society is a meritocracy - that is a society with unspecified levels of inequality, but with equal opportunities to compete for advantageous positions within it. Michael Young coined the term meritocracy in 1958 as the title of his dystopian satire *The Rise of the Meritocracy*. The point of this book, as Young reiterated in an article in 2001 shortly before he died, is that meritocracy is unworkable. It depends on the upward mobility of talented individuals from poorer backgrounds, and on the downward mobility of dimmer richer people. The latter is blocked by the fact that privileged groups will go to any lengths to prevent their less able children dropping very far down the social hierarchy. Furthermore, as Young argued, a system in which the least well off are forced to attribute their position to their personal inadequacy rather than to bad luck or injustice would in fact generate resentment and rebellion, thus making the system inherently unstable. Most importantly, though, meritocratic arguments are intrinsically inegalitarian. As Hattersley once said, talk of ladders of opportunity presumes the continuing existence of the pits.

The pragmatic argument against meritocracy is that you cannot, in fact, have equality of opportunity when there are large substantive inequalities. The problem is the privilege of the rich as well as the deprivation of the poor. Emile Durkheim, a not very radical sociologist, suggested over a hundred years ago that equality of opportunity was inconsistent with inherited wealth. Compass, however, like most contemporary commentators and policy makers is primarily concerned with the inequity of poverty. Of course, as William Morris wrote, 'making a great many poor people, or even a few, somewhat more comfortable than they are now ... is not in itself a light good'. However, even if the 22 per cent of the population (down from 25 per cent in 1996/7) below 60 per cent of median income were raised out of poverty, the problem of the rich would remain. There cannot be equal opportunities when a section of the population can buy privilege in health care and in education, when extreme wealth distorts housing markets, and when such wealth misdirects social labour to the production of - as Morris put it - 'sordid makeshifts' for people who cannot afford better, and 'luxuries for rich folk, the greater part of which even their personal folly does not make them want'. Will Hutton is the only contemporary commentator to consistently address the problem of the rich, their self-exclusion from 'mainstream society' and the consequences of this for the quality of public services.

Compass fails to make even this strong pragmatic case for greater substantive equality as the necessary foundation of equality of opportunity. Rather, it argues that 'investment in pre-school children ... is the most effective way of giving children genuine equality of opportunity'. More fundamentally, the basic principle of a meritocracy (or equal opportunity to be unequal) runs counter to any meaningful concept of equal worth. It is perhaps possible for those who are religious to believe in equal worth in the sight of God, independently of the worth placed on individuals by the society in which they live. For those of us who, like Wordsworth, believe that this world is the place 'where in the end we find our happiness or not at all', this is not an option. The justification of inequality in a meritocratic system rests on the assertion that some people are - literally - *worth more* than others. That is, they are *not* of equal worth. The basis for this unequal worth in Young's satire was the equation 'IQ plus effort equals merit', effectively translated by New Labour as talent plus work equals merit. But innate capacities are not a matter of merit, they are a matter of luck. Their development into skills and capacities is a social process, dependent always on the nurture, care, skills and capacities of others. Occupying a social location that permits this - globally and historically speaking a somewhat rare privilege - does not self-evidently generate an entitlement to a larger than average share of the social product.

If equality of opportunity is understood not as equal opportunity to compete, but an equal opportunity of human wellbeing and development of capacities, it becomes hard to justify unequal access to resources of any kind. Richard Wilkinson's work has shown that this is quite literally a matter of life and death. Levels of inequality in society - not just poverty and deprivation - have an adverse effect on overall mortality rates. A broad understanding of equality of opportunity, understood as the equal opportunity to survive and flourish, leads inexorably in the direction of equality of condition. It is often argued that substantive equality is inimical to liberty and diversity and involves the imposition of uniformity - an objection embedded in the term 'equality of outcome'. Compass is very clear that the antithesis between equality and liberty is false: 'equality is not the enemy of liberty but the means of pursuing it', and 'without equality there is freedom only for some'. But it is less clear on the relationship between equality and diversity, presenting pluralism and equality as antagonistic principles in need of reconciliation. Yet equal access to the means of self-development should allow more positive diversity, as more people's talents find expression. Not all kinds of difference and diversity are good, but a genuine social pluralism not born of ascribed and imposed differences would also be fostered rather than suppressed by equality of condition.

This might imply a very different kind of society. At the end of the Compass document, there is a gesture in this direction, and a suggestion that there are irreconcilable antagonisms between capitalism and sustainability (and therefore human need): 'making environmental sustainability an organising principle of modern life will mean reappraising the dominant model of economic development;' and 'ultimately a truly ambitious environmental policy will take us into new political territory'. But this political territory, when and if we get there, does not automatically imply greater equality: it will need to be argued and struggled for. In the meantime, we need to recognise that global capitalism is a system essentially driven by the logic of profit and capital accumulation, which has nothing to do with human need or equality at all.

William Morris once said that social democratic measures were either a 'makeshift alleviation to help us through the present days of oppression' or a 'means for landing us in the new country of equality'. Strong forms of social democracy can at least provide the former, and have in the past delivered much lower levels of inequality in Britain than we now have. Arguments for equality will always be weak and equivocal when they accommodate to, rather than challenge, neo-liberalism; and a social democracy that does not seriously address questions of the ownership and control of productive property cannot (re)instate egalitarianism as a core political value.

Customer-focused government

Catherine Needham

Catherine Needham *argues that to see public service users as customers is to impoverish the notion of citizenship.*

Twenty-five years of neo-liberal politics in Britain have transformed the citizen into a consumer. Both supporters and critics of neo-liberalism acknowledge this metamorphosis. For those who support the policies of Thatcher, Major and Blair, the citizen-consumer symbolises their rejection of producerism with its overtones of trade unionism and bureaucratic waste. Critics of neo-liberalism, however, have seen the recasting of the citizen as a consumer as part of a broader agenda of marketisation and depoliticisation. As Stuart Hall noted in issue 24 of *Soundings*, 'The reduction of the citizen to consumer, and the "privatisation of need" is at the centre of the market model'. Alan Finlayson in the same issue argued that the public choice theories underpinning Labour's approach replaced the political role of citizen with the economic role of consumer.

For both advocates and critics of neo-liberalism the citizen-consumer is a bundle of abstractions - embodying self-determination, power and status on the one side, and individualism, selfishness and manipulation on the other. Consumerisation is seen by both sides as a feature of the broader importation of private sector attributes into the public sector. Yet neither side is explicit about what it means to treat the citizen as a consumer: does it mean to recast the citizen in the role of rational economic actor as in abstract public choice models, or is it to engage with all the complexities of being a real-life consumer? Both these variants constitute a distortion of citizenship, but they do not necessarily have the same manifestations or implications. The citizen as abstract economic actor is empowered within a marketplace but forfeits the political dimension of citizenship. The citizen as real-life consumer is also depoliticised, and may also have a weak market position in the face of bewildering choice and poor information. These complexities within the consumer role need to be addressed.

It is also important to recognise that the citizen-consumer is not just an analytic abstraction, but - in the guise of customer - is alive, well and living in the performance plans and customer charters of central and local government. Politicians, civil servants and local government officers increasingly boast that government is becoming 'customer-focused'. The significance of this cannot be over-estimated. Government does not treat its citizens as consumers only in an abstract sense. It explicitly designates its service users as customers. This has tremendous implications for the way that those who work in and use public services feel about them.

Three variants of consumerisation

What does it mean to treat someone as a customer or a consumer? The Conservative reforms of public services and management in the 1980s and 1990s generated a cottage industry of academic literature discussing the extent to which the citizen had been cast in the role of consumer. From early commentaries on new public management through to the Citizen's Charter, the appropriateness of introducing consumerist modes of behaviour into the public sector was analysed. There were different assumptions about what it meant to treat someone as a consumer. These included providing service with a smile, offering choice and competition on a par with the private sector, and treating the individual as one who 'consumes' rather than 'produces' politics. For some authors, to be a consumer was to be one who uses goods and services, without prejudging the terms on which they are used; for others, to label someone a consumer was to make assumptions about the bases on which they chose goods and exercised power. The lack of consistency in the term consumer is seen by some as weakening its power as an explanatory variable. In fact, through exploring the different ways in which citizens can be treated as consumers, it is possible to trace the continuities and differences between New Labour's approach to government and that of its Conservative predecessors.

The ambiguities surrounding consumerisation reflect three divergent strands within analyses of consumerism - the neo-classical economic approaches, the more sociologically inspired conceptions, and intermediate liberal approaches. In the economic model the consumer is a market actor, exercising choice; in the liberal model the consumer is equipped with rights to compensate for the inequities or information asymmetries of the market; in the sociological model, consumer behaviour is socially constructed, and the consumer is vulnerable to social pressures to consume and conform. Through exploring these three conceptions of the consumer in more detail it is possible to see the shifting emphases of recent UK governments.

The approaches categorised as economic derive their understanding of the consumer from economic theory, particularly the neo-classical approach in which the consumer plays a central role. Building on utilitarian theories, neo-classical economics depicts the consumer as a rational utility maximiser, with stable, exogenous preferences, revealed through the act of choice. Choice is constrained only through individual resources and product availability. As Elster argues, 'The consumer chooses between courses of action that differ only in the way that they affect him.'[1] Control of the choice set is through aggregate signalling, rather than concerted action. Consumers 'do not participate in decisions concerning the products they buy except in choosing whether or not to buy it.'[2] Producers and suppliers are engaged in a bilateral relationship based on voluntary exchange only for the duration of the transaction. When applied to public services, these economic models assume that public sector transactions have the characteristics of their private sector counterparts: choice, competition, individualism, a given set of preferences and market accountability. The citizen-consumer is a rational utility maximiser. This is the approach taken by public choice theorists, as Finlayson highlighted in *Soundings* 24.

The liberal conception of the consumer has its roots in the consumer rights

1. J. Elster, 'The Market and the Forum: Three Varieties of Political Theory', in R.E. Goodin and P. Pettit (ed), *Contemporary Political Philosophy: An Anthology*, Blackwell 1997, p132.
2. H. Elcock, 'What Price Citizenship? Public Management and the Citizen's Charter', in J.A. Chandler (ed), *The Citizen's Charter*, Dartmouth 1996, p31.

movement. This perspective draws on the economic role of consumer, but engages critically with this model's assumptions of consumer responsiveness, and recognises the need to protect the consumer within the market place. It is a liberal conception in the sense that the state intervenes in the market to enforce contracts and protect consumers. This view of the public sector consumer is the one invoked by Prior et al: 'The citizen is empowered as a consumer by being given specific rights: to receive information on standards and performance of services, to have individual needs assessed, to assert choices and preferences, to complain and to receive redress.'[3] Beyond enumerated rights, consumers may have certain entitlements such as being treated with respect. For the citizen-consumer, this model simulates in the public sector the 'customer care' approach which profit-seeking creates within the private sector. Through the provision of information and the extension of consultation mechanisms, upward accountability to elected politicians is supplemented by downward accountability to service providers.

Missing from the economic and liberal approaches to the citizen-consumer is any conception of consumerism as a social phenomenon. Sociological theories, in contrast, reject the utilitarian assumptions that economic theories make about people and provide a view of the individual informed by 'culture not calculus'.[4] Emphasis is placed not only on the use value of commodities, but also on the cultural significance of consumption. Preferences are assumed to be shaped in the social context of consumption rather than being fixed and exogenous. Since in the sociological model preferences are culturally informed, consumers become vulnerable to manipulation through advertising. In a situation where consumers are reliant for information on promotional material from a company, and where market research data is used to measure the susceptibility of the consumer to particular messages, a consumer's preferences may match the agenda of the company rather than her own interests. The citizen-consumer, in this sociological model, is therefore one who may be manipulated by the promotional techniques of government, or may be a passive recipient of government messages rather

3. D. Prior, J. Stewart, and K. Walsh, *Citizenship: Rights, Community and Participation*, Pitman 1995, p15.
4. P. Hall and R. Taylor, 'Political Science and the Three New Institutionalisms', *Political Studies*, Vol. 44, No. 5, 1996.

than an active participant in politics.

Thus the citizen-consumer is a multidimensional figure, seen by some analysts as an empowered individual exercising choice, by others as a bearer of rights, and by a third group as a social creature, vulnerable to manipulation. These attributes are not only different; they are to an extent contradictory. The model of the passive, manipulated consumer can be seen as the opposite of the empowered consumer, armed with a package of rights. Yet it is also important to note that these approaches share a common core: across all variants of the citizen-consumer, the citizen is presumed to mimic a private sector consumer and stands in the same relation to public goods, services and providers as her private sector equivalent.

Has citizenship been consumerised?

Surveying the governments of Thatcher, Major and Blair, it is possible to find traces of all these forms of consumerisation, although the balance has shifted between administrations. The economic model, based on expanding choice to the citizen-consumer, enjoyed rhetorical support under the Conservatives. The consumer as economic actor was held up as a model of empowerment. The Conservatives' 1987 manifesto heralded, 'a capital-owning democracy', and promised 'a profound and progressive transformation - popular capitalism'. Choice was expanded in education (in terms of different types of schools), but primarily the Conservatives emphasised the exit right of citizens, allowing them to escape from public services - through right to buy schemes, nursery vouchers and tax incentives for private health care. Furthermore, the internal market introduced into health between purchaser and provider offered little new choice to the individual user. Indeed, since patients were discouraged from seeking care from providers that did not hold contracts with their 'home' purchasers, it actually limited patient choice of specialists.

The liberal model of the consumer was central to the Citizen's Charter initiative introduced under Major. The charter approach sought to provide a public sector equivalent of the statutory rights of private sector consumers, acting to defend users in areas where the market did not assure service quality. Users of public services were furnished with rights to basic levels of service, such as a limited waiting time at a hospital. League tables and performance indicators gave users the opportunity to compare the treatment they were receiving with the promised level. Consultation with users about desired and experienced level of service was a key element of the charter approach. However, the Citizen's Charter, and its many spin-offs, came under sustained attack, for its narrow definition of rights and emaciated vision of the citizen. It offered managerial answers to public service shortcomings rather than engaging with the political dimensions of citizenship.

As Stuart Hall noted in *Soundings* 24, New Labour's tendency at the beginning of its first term of office was to demonise public services; only later - with schools and the NHS becoming a bad news story for the government - did it shift towards a commitment to service improvement. Since then its vision of reformed public services has been one which draws explicitly on the notion of the citizen as a consumer, exercising choice in the same way as her private sector counterpart. Choice has been expanded in a number of areas, from elective operations to social care payments and social housing allocation. In these services, money follows the user, for example through 'payment by results' in the NHS, where hospitals will receive funding on the basis of how many patients they can attract. The citizen as economic consumer is a key figure in New Labour's second term approach.

The charters and their rights-based discourse have not survived under New Labour. In some areas, such as health, charters have been replaced by documents that put much more emphasis on the responsibilities of users than on their rights. Within local government, many authorities have some form of charter, but they talk of 'promises' to 'customers' rather than the 'rights' of 'citizens'. New Labour's alternative to the rights approach has been an emphasis on the subjective needs of the user. The professional assessment of need that underpinned both the traditional welfare state approach and the charter initiative has been replaced by an approach that claims to customise services around the 'felt needs' of the user. Rather than government devising a set of rights for all service users, the emphasis has been on users themselves expressing what they want from services. This personalisation agenda is linked to the choice approach. In social housing, health and social care, for example, users are supposed to be able to shape the service around their own needs, according to the choices that they make.

Even in areas where choice is not being extended, staff are being encouraged to be as sensitive as possible to the needs of individual users. Customer Relationship Management software, adapted from the private sector, allows local councils to provide a much more individualised service to users. As one local government officer put it: 'It's just a big database of customers who we've provided service to … In the fullness of time we should have the information for segmenting our market, so that we understand how to deal with different parts of the market better and more responsively.'[5] In place of the charter rights, weak though they were, New Labour offers market segmentation and customer care.

The sociological/cultural approach to the consumer emphasises that consumers do not necessarily act as rational utility maximisers with exogenous preferences, but are susceptible to having their preferences manipulated. Thus the use of promotional forms of information by both the Conservatives and New Labour raises concerns that the citizen-consumer is subject to the same distortions. Both consultation and information can be seen as tools that have been used strategically by recent government to maximise popular consent for their proposals. The Conservatives drew heavy criticism for advertising which promoted controversial policies such as privatisation, the poll tax and the Citizen's Charter before Parliament had chance to consider them. Bernard Ingham, Thatcher's press secretary, became notorious for his robust efforts to make the news agenda reflect the interests of his patron.

The promotional aspects of government information have been formalised under New Labour, with the creation of new structures and guidelines for government communicators. Promotional forms of information aim not to inform citizens about a particular issue but to ensure that the government 'message' is received by citizens with minimum distortion. This is partly about using old propaganda techniques of rhetoric and bluster to convince the public of the government's case. It is also about utilising commercial techniques such as branding and marketing, which have explicit 'selling' aims. The Central Office of Information, for example, describes itself on its website as, 'the government's independent centre of excellence and expertise for marketing communications'. In this marketing approach, Stuart Hall is right to note that 'spin' is more than just the froth on top of the government's approach. It is crucial to the government's sales driven agenda, in which information is used to increase New Labour's 'market share'.

---

5. This interview was part of research conducted in eight local authorities, selected to give a spread of council types and regions within England. Three officers were interviewed from each of the eight local authorities.

The marketing focus of New Labour is evident not only from its approach to government information, but also from the way it consults with citizens. New Labour has expanded the use of consultation at central and local government level. Answers to parliamentary questions indicate that departments are doing more social research and consultation than ever before. A substantial proportion of this research involves measuring user 'satisfaction'. At local government level in particular, performance indicators are frequently based on a quantifiable user satisfaction score. In this utilitarian approach the aggregation of individual feelings of satisfaction becomes the measure of government success. Leaving aside concerns with the methodology of satisfaction measurement, which is insensitive to the different expectations that users may have of a service, such an approach conceives of public services as nothing more than vehicles to satisfy individual users. Collective goals such as redistribution, public health and the wider public good have no place in this landscape of individual preferences. Methods of consultation which limit public participation to customer satisfaction surveys give the impression of involving the citizen whilst doing nothing to stimulate real engagement.

'"spin" is crucial to the government's sales driven agenda, in which information is used to increase New Labour's market share'

Surveying almost twenty-five years of neo-liberal governments it is possible to find all variants of the citizen-consumer role: economic, liberal and sociological. But under New Labour, user choice, customisation of services and manipulation of responses have all intensified. The public face of the government is utilitarian - user satisfaction is the measure of success within public services. As Blair put it: 'Customer satisfaction has to become a culture, a way of life, not an "added extra"'.[6] This utilitarian approach is interesting, given that Blair himself has disavowed utilitarianism in the past: 'I think there is a danger sometimes that we look at everything just in terms of what its utilitarian value is,' he said in a 2001 interview with *The Economist*. Yet New Labour's approach is highly utilitarian in some senses, with customer satisfaction policed by an army of regulators, and a 'what matters is what works' mantra driving the government agenda. This utilitarianism is evident in New Labour's shift away from the language of rights in relation to service

6. T. Blair, *The Courage of Our Convictions: why reform of the public services is the route to social justice*, Fabian Society 2002, p5.

delivery, towards choice and customer satisfaction. Yet for New Labour satisfaction is not the exogenous variable that the classic utilitarians envisaged. Rather New Labour seeks to manipulate responses through misleading information and through offering minimal opportunities to debate the standards against which satisfaction is to be measured.

The redesignation of the citizen as customer

The consumerisation of citizenship under New Labour is evident not only from its broad approach to public service reform, but also from the language the government uses to refer to service users. Since New Labour came to power, and particularly since the 2001 election, a linguistic revolution has occurred. The user of public services is no longer a citizen, a user, a client, nor even a consumer. In the argot of the Office of Public Service Reform (OPSR), the Cabinet Secretary and a series of government white papers, public services must be focused on their 'customers'. In 2002, the OPSR launched the government's *Principles of Public Service Reform*, which stated that 'for investment to deliver the improvements wanted, public services will have to be rebuilt round the needs of their customers' (www.pm.gov.uk/files/pdf/Principles.pdf, p8). At the head of the civil service, Cabinet Secretary Andrew Turnbull publicly stated his commitment to this customer-orientation. In 2001, in an article in the civil service magazine *Connect*, he wrote, 'That is now the strategic goal of our delivery and reform agenda - to transform public services and ensure that we deliver customer-centred services' (www.cmps.gov.uk). This language is now commonly used in ministerial speeches and government white papers. Delivering 'customer-focused' services is a core aim of central government.

Similar patterns are evident within local government, where a customer approach has taken a strong hold. Thus in my study of eight local authorities, document analysis and interviews with officers revealed a commitment to this customer orientation. Best Value Performance Plans were found to contain four times as many references to customers as to citizens. On their websites several of the councils had customer charters, a linguistic shift that makes Major's citizen's charters seem imbued with civic meaning. Officers in these councils, almost without exception, said that they found the language of customer helpful. As one put it: 'I think we have to see those we are communicating with as our customers, and have that kind of relationship and respect for them as our customers.' Front-line staff within councils were being retrained as 'customer care' professionals.

The citizen as customer is the real-life manifestation of consumerisation. Customer-focused government is increasingly the model which policy-makers mandate and service staff apply. The private sector provider-customer relationship is the model to which front-line workers are expected to conform. A clear illustration of this is given in a guide to improving local government communications produced by the Office of the Deputy Prime Minister and Local Government Association. One of the 'frequently asked questions' states:

Q: Why all this concern with 'brand identity' or 'reputation management'? We're not Nike or Tesco.

A: Councils aren't private companies. But the principles of and rationale for brand and reputation management are the same: clear, consistent messages, a professional and recognisable 'look and feel' to communications, and the credibility that comes from delivering on your promise to the customer.[7]

That such a goal should animate local government communicators is deeply troubling for those who see information as a key facilitator of democratic participation.

This explicit designation of the service user as a customer marks an intensification of the consumer orientation. New Labour's rationale for this shift is a combination of desirability and inevitability. An approach that treats service users as customers is seen as desirable because it raises satisfaction levels, improves efficiency, enhances equity and keeps the middle classes wedded to public provision. The local government officers I interviewed believed that calling people customers was desirable because it symbolised a cultural shift within councils. It signified that councils were committed to providing a high quality service that responded to the needs of local people.

At both central and local government level there is a sense that not only are these changes desirable, they are also inevitable. Blair's speeches on public services warn of ever more demanding consumers, whose expectations are shaped

7.   Improvement and Development Agency (IDEA), *Connecting with Communities: Improving Communications in Local Government*, 2002 www.idea-knowledge.gov.uk.

by their private sector experiences. He talks of a 'consumer age' and 'consumer society', conveying the sense that these are widely recognised phenomena, and beyond the scope of government to resist. The local government interviewees too felt that people came to the council with expectations shaped by private sector experiences. As one put it: 'Things like call centres, bank call centres, phone banking - you can phone them any time, bank online. I think people expect that of their councils now.' Councils were seen as having no choice but to respond to these new expectations.

Such attitudes feed into what Stuart Hall, in *Soundings* 24, called a new consumer-focused, free market 'common sense'. The dominant ideology of consumerisation makes opposition to New Labour's approach seem perverse. To be against their reforms is to be in favour of insensitive bureaucracy, to be against services which match the needs of their users. It is, most persuasively, to be against the inevitable march of a 'consumer society' to which governments have no option but to submit.

Loyalty and public service

Yet for those who do not fetishise the private sector, the limitations of treating a citizen as a consumer are clear. Models of delivery, payment and choice in the public sector are far more complex than their private sector equivalents. Citizens may use services they do not pay for and pay for services they do not use; they may be unwilling or involuntary users, or may not know what kind of service they need; they may demand a service but be denied it due to rationing or ineligibility. The limits on competition in the public sector make it difficult for the citizen to exit when faced with an unsatisfactory service. Even where governments are introducing 'customer care' in order to increase responsiveness to users, rather than as a form of direct marketisation, there are limits to the extent to which public services can respond to the subjective needs of users. Professional assessment of need will continue to restrict access to public services, given limited supply and high demand.

These limitations are related to the different structures of private and public services, and are fairly well rehearsed.[8] To these critiques must be added a new

---

8. See C. Hood, *Administrative Analysis*, Harvester Wheatsheaf 1986; and C. Needham, *Citizen-Consumers: New Labour's Marketplace Democracy*, Catalyst 2003.

tranche of concerns about the effects of instructing people to think of themselves as customers when they use public services. This amounts to telling people that insofar as they get good quality service in the public sector, it is because they are customers. Being a citizen is simply not enough. Yet how can those same people be encouraged to accept the collective responsibilities of citizenship - to participate in democratic structures, to contribute to redistributive taxation - when everything they get back from the state they get as customers not citizens? Some argue that treating people well as customers of government is an essential pre-requisite to encouraging them to engage as citizens. But it is not at all clear why high levels of customer satisfaction would stimulate political activity. If people are encouraged to think of themselves as customers of public services, then issues of democracy and the public good become as peripheral to the public sector as they are to the private.

Rather than encouraging people to participate, calling them customers may be eroding the loyalty on which such services depend. One of the most elegant models of the relationship between service users and providers is the famous account offered by Albert Hirschman in his book *Exit, Voice and Loyalty* (1970). In this model citizens - and private sector consumers - are expected to balance exit, voice and loyalty in their relationships with service providers. Dissatisfied consumers are likely primarily to resort to exit, moving to another supplier; citizens will use voice, to raise problems and work for improvement. Loyalty ties people in to their existing provider, creating a sense that it is worth striving for improvement, rather than taking the exit option.

The problem with New Labour's model of customer-focused government is that it emphasises exit (choice) and voice (user consultation) and fails to recognise the importance of loyalty. Public services can only flourish where they inspire a sense of loyalty from their users. People need to believe in the collective goals of public service - which extend beyond the individualised needs of users. Public health services require that people minimise trivial claims on doctors and look after their own health. Welfare payments require low social tolerance of fraud. Schools benefit if parents encourage children to do homework. Yet the sense of collective endeavour and self-restraint is alien to the customer. Customers push their maximal claims because that is essence of the market relationship. Encouraging the users of public services to consider themselves as customers risks eroding the sense of loyalty that underpins the whole notion of public service.

Similar concerns attach to those that work in public services. The redesignation of citizens as customers must be dispiriting to those whose commitment to and enthusiasm for their job comes from a sense that there is something *different* about public services. The public service ethos that attracts many workers into public sector employment runs counter to the current marketisation and consumerisation of the government-citizen relationship. The difficult decisions that social workers, doctors and housing officers have to make in rationing their services are not made easier by casting the recipient in the position of an expectant customer. If front-line workers are encouraged to think of their users as customers there is a real risk that something valuable in that relationship will be lost.

To stress the importance of loyalty and ethos is not to require public service users to take what they get and be grateful for it; nor is it to make public service workers tolerate poor pay and conditions. Rather it is to recognise that the limitations of consumerist approaches extend beyond the problem of the false analogies they make between public and private modes of distribution. Customer language threatens to corrode the very presumptions on which public service depend.

This may be exactly what New Labour intends. Services are easier to parcel out to the private sector if people can no longer remember why it was important for them to be public. User responsiveness in public services becomes a way to enhance a broader agenda of marketisation. In the Blairite approach, public services have no alternative but to strive for private sector standards of customer care, and when they fail by these standards they are condemned and part-privatised. Such a catch-22 leaves public servants and service users gasping for a democratic defence of public services. An apparently self-evident point must be reaffirmed: we need to be treated well in the public sector not because we are customers but because we are citizens. We need to treat our public services well because they symbolise what we believe in as citizens not what we demand as customers.

Rethinking audit and inspection

Michael Rustin

Michael Rustin *criticises the dominant systems of public service audit, arguing that they are undermining belief in the public sector. He proposes instead more constructive forms of inspection, which place emphasis on working together for improvement rather than on regulation through sanctions and competition.*

It has become conventional wisdom since the beginning of New Labour's second term that the government's success depends on whether it can bring about tangible improvements in public services, such as health, education, and transport. It has gone about the task through significant increases in spending, and by establishing a draconian regime of target-setting, regulation and inspection. Its methods of managing the public sector have largely followed precedents established by previous Conservative governments, in its commitment to market mechanisms wherever these can be introduced, and to central regulatory controls where they can't. Alan Finlayson, in recent issues of *Soundings* (23 and 24) and in his *Making Sense of New Labour* (2003), has documented the ideology of 'modernisation' and the doctrines of 'new public management' which underpin its policies.[1]

This article argues that this approach is self-destructive in many respects. The government, and Tony Blair in particular, are seeking to 'rescue' and 'modernise' the public sector by, so to speak, campaigning against much of what it actually is and does. This ceaseless critique erodes public confidence in the very idea of a public sector even while the government is supposedly demonstrating that it alone can make it work. Its continuous criticism and fault-finding also has the effect of alienating the public sector workforce, which becomes defensive and fearful when it should be the government's most enthusiastic ally in the search for improvement. In particular, the article examines the 'micro-regimes' of regulation which have become so important to the government's 'delivery strategy', and the pervasive systems of audit and inspection which now plague every inch of the public sector - to which huge resources of money and time are being diverted, away from the primary services themselves. I argue against the goals of competitive ranking and 'consumer choice' which unduly dominate these audits and inspections. I propose instead that these procedures should be designed to facilitate improvement, innovation and learning, and to create alliances between service providers, service-users, and citizens in support of public goods that all can identify with. Only if there is a change in the present systems of regulation of these services can public confidence in them be restored, and the idea of the public good on which social democracy depends be renewed.

Audit and inspection

Audit and Inspection has become an increasingly important element in the operation of the public services in the last decade or so, as everyone who works in these services well knows. OFSTED, CHI (shortly to become CHAI), QUAHE, SSI, HM Inspectorate of Prisons - there is an inspectorate for each field of public services, with the Audit Commission itself at the top of this hierarchy, with its broader remit and responsibility for local government. There are also the inspection agencies - OFCOM, OFWAT et al - which emerged to

---

1. In a valuable discussion of 'new public management', Alan Finlayson (*Making Sense of New Labour*, Lawrence and Wishart 2003) has contrasted an earlier civil service model of bureaucratic hierarchy and probity with new systems which devolve responsibility to separate units and sub-agencies, and devise measures which enable managers at these dispersed or subordinate levels to be controlled at a distance. Inspection regimes are a key part of this new management system. The devolution of responsibilities to managers, with devolved budgets as a prime instrument, passes responsibility to them while denying them support. Such regimes often involve 'de-layering' or stripping out levels of management. In effect these assumptions undermine the idea that containing and supportive structures are what sustain good practice, and substitute models which depend on reward and punishment.

regulate formerly public but now private infrastructural industries. In 1994 Michael Power published a widely-noticed Demos pamphlet, *The Audit Explosion*, which drew attention to this burgeoning phenomenon, and pointed out the discrepancy between the claims made for it and the evidence for its effectiveness. In 2002, Onora O'Neill's Reith Lectures, published under the title *A Question of Trust*, drew attention to the distrust of professionals inherent in the rise of the regulatory culture, and gave a measured dissenting voice to the professional employees who have felt themselves to be primary targets of the new inspection system, including of course academics. The choice of this topic and of its lecturer by the BBC were a sensitive index of the level of concern and opposition which these new regulatory systems have evoked in what one could describe as 'middle Britain', though this is not quite what Tony Blair means by this term.

In the face of criticism and resistance in the various public services, there has of late been some softening of the methods and approaches adopted to inspection and audit, in its largest spheres of education and health. There is talk of a 'lighter touch' by inspectors, and of the earning of partial exemption from the most rigorous inspecting routines for institutions that meet various criteria of quality in first audits. The conversion of CHI, the Commission for Health Improvement, into CHAI, the Commission for Healthcare Audit and Inspection, is accompanied by new broader aims and guidelines which look likely to be an improvement on those of CHI, whose focus on 'governance' (i.e. administrative procedures) was unduly narrow from the start. But there is little evidence that there has been any fundamental rethinking of purpose in these modifications of practice. It seems rather that the aim is to reduce the levels of conflict with institutions, also perhaps the burgeoning direct and indirect costs produced by these systems, while preserving their essential character. The question is, are such minor changes enough? Is the current system of audit, regulation and inspection founded on sound principles? Have alternative ways of conceiving and operating the system been put forward and debated? I shall suggest in this article that they have not, but should be.

Origins and purposes of inspection systems

The origins of our present systems plainly lie in part in the deep distrust of public service provision by the Conservative governments of the 1980s and 1990s. Public services were regarded by them as unaccountable to the public or to consumers, and as having been 'captured' by producer interests, both professional and trade union. The lack of 'consumer choice' in the delivery of many public services was contrasted with its importance in the spheres of private consumption. The absence of the disciplines of competition and the market were noted as an inefficient aspect of public provision. Some important goods were transferred in bulk by the Thatcher government from the public to the private sectors, notably council housing, through the 'right to buy' legislation. But government recognised that other services, such as school, health, and social services, could not easily be privatised, whether for political or operational reasons. Alternative strategies were therefore developed, either to bring market or quasi-market disciplines to bear on these services ('internal markets' in the NHS, compulsory tendering in local government), or to bring about greater public accountability for their performance. Inspection and audit systems were the principal means chosen for achieving this greater public accountability. However, by establishing common and public measures of performance and relative merit ('league tables' and the award of 'stars') these audit systems were also used to enhance and enforce competition, by increasing the information available to individual consumers to make their choices of service-provider.

Inspection and audit systems can have - and indeed usually combine - a number of different purposes. One of the problems of recent British systems is that their development seems to have been accompanied by no significant public debate about what these different purposes might be. Although one of the main principles which justifies the entire regulatory system is the necessity for 'evidence-based practice', the regulatory system seems itself to have developed with little interest in the evidence of its effectiveness. One would have expected such an important engine of government to have been developed by means of a lengthy process of experiment, research, and debate, but this has not been the case.[2]

---

2. One of the principal influences on the development of audit regimes in the public sector has been movements for quality assurance and 'total quality management' in the manufacturing industry, and subsequently in other fields of business. Here also changes have been propagated by charismatic advocates - management educators and ideas-people - but they have mostly not been warranted, as scientific innovations would have been, by empirical research. Thus questions remain about the transferability of such methods from their source-contexts. See Adrian Wilkinson and Hugh Colin (eds), *Making Quality Critical*, Routledge 1995; and Colin Morgan and Stephen Murgatroyd, *Total Quality Management in the Public Sector*, Open University Press 1994.

We could identify the legitimate goals of these inspection systems as broadly falling into three categories: raising common agreed standards of performance; measuring comparative performance; and improving quality.

Raising common standards

Ensuring that common agreed standards of performance and output are met by institutions and their sub-units is a substantial undertaking in itself. It requires that such standards and objectives are first determined and agreed, and then specified in terms which enable their achievement to be reliably measured.

In some areas of provision, such as primary education, anxiety that such standards and objectives were not being widely met was a shaping influence on the inspection system. The development of the National Curriculum and its various component devices (the national literacy and numeracy hours, etc), and the devising of earlier and more frequent Key Stage assessments, were closely associated with the development of the OFSTED inspection regime, one of whose purposes was to ensure that the goals specified by these measures were fulfilled by all schools.

But in other areas of provision, such as university education, the aim of ensuring that agreed common standards were met was a rather weak justification for the elaborate systems introduced. There seemed little reason for general concern about academic standards in universities at the time when the current Quality Assurance regime was introduced. And, once instituted, the inspection regime began to find that the vast majority of programmes and institutions inspected were achieving standards deemed to be satisfactory or better. The dire effects of the 40 per cent reduction in funding-per-student over twenty years then passed unnoticed by the inspection system, and has only now been acknowledged as a problem to justify top-up fees.

In the sphere of health, it has proved more difficult to define and determine what acceptable standards and goals of provision are, since these depend on complex measures of rates of mortality and recovery, and on the relative costs of treatment in systems which are necessarily very different from one another. A health service is a conglomerate of specialisms related to each other in complex networks of co-operation and interdependency, not a unified production system producing an easily standardised or classifiable output. The 'outputs' of such systems are millions of individual patients or ex-patients, not composite products like Toyota cars or Boeing aircraft. If there is a defective element in the production system for a vehicle, it is going to degrade the standard of the whole product, perhaps fatally. But although specialisms are interdependent in health systems, it is unlikely to be obvious how the output of a whole system is being affected by its different parts. It is perhaps partly for this reason that the inspection and accountability systems in the NHS have so far devoted so much of their attention to secondary measures of quality, such as 'waiting lists', or to procedural measures, such as 'governance', rather than to the measures that matter most, such as the effectiveness and cost of treatments. The medical profession does manifest its keen interest in the latter in the pages of *The Lancet* and the *British Medical Journal*, but methods of comparative medical audit are still resisted.

Where public services deal with populations who are in some respect 'residual' in their characteristics, as opposed to those representing a cross-section of the people (like health, schools and universities), their inspection systems have different priorities. In Her Majesty's Prisons, and in the Social Services, the achievement of adequate minimum standards has been a matter of constant concern for inspectors. The Reports of HM Inspectorate of Prisons, under its three most recent Chief Inspectors (Stephen Tumim 1987-95, David Ramsbotham 1995-2001, Anne Owers 2001 to the present), record an ongoing struggle by the Inspectors to define and enforce acceptable standards for the prison service. This has been against the thrust of criminal justice policy under the three most recent Home Secretaries - Michael Howard, Jack Straw, and David Blunkett - since all of them have sought to increase the numbers of offenders imprisoned, whereas the Chief Inspectors have all argued that they should be substantially reduced.

In Social Services, the routine systems of inspection by SSI have been repeatedly overshadowed by a different regulatory method, namely the special Committees of Inquiry set up in response to specific high profile cases - in particular incidences of failure by the child care services whose purpose is to protect the lives and well-being of individual children. The Victoria Climbié Inquiry is the latest example of these. But it seems unlikely that the investigation of single catastrophes, however meticulous, can provide sound evidence on which to be base social policies. The government seems happy to demand that professionals adopt evidence-based practices, while their own interventions seem more often driven by ideology or expediency.

Measuring comparative performance

A second objective of current systems is to define and measure the relative or comparative performance of providers of services. This has been accomplished by devising indicators of quality, and by transforming necessarily qualitative measures into numerical indicators, thus making possible the 'scoring' and 'ranking' of institutions and services. The inspection systems themselves have sometimes been somewhat coy about this aspect of their work. For example, in their oral report to those in a university they have just inspected, QUAHE inspectors have been known to decline the suggestion to add up the separate scores from their six separate areas of assessment into a composite score, even though everyone knows that the composite score is the item of most acute concern to everyone. But no-one has been deceived by this reluctance to take note of the obvious - what can be added up, will be added up. So now 'league tables' have an extremely important part in both the school and university systems, partly through the role of the press. This has been justified on grounds of enhanced 'consumer choice'. It is claimed that if publics know which are good schools or universities, and which are bad, they will be able to choose the good, and avoid the bad. So, in effect, a new and improved market has been created, in which league table positions, constructed from various indicators and reports of inspections, allow objective measures of 'product quality' to be obtained. Monetary prices to consumers remain for the moment out of this quasi-market, since most health and education services are still provided without charge at the point of use. But the enhanced top-up fees proposed for universities will weaken this principle, and it is possible that once Foundation Hospitals are established, with their greater autonomy, they will eventually be permitted to allow their customers to pay for 'top-up' services of extra quality.

The NHS audit systems have so far mainly relied on a star system rather than on a serial ranking of Trusts. Those with 'three stars' qualify for particular financial benefits, and for exemptions from certain kinds of regulation; a 'three star' ranking is also a precondition for Foundation Status. However, comparative rankings and league tables have begun to emerge from various sources. Since the measures on which these rankings are based are largely secondary to the primary task of the Trusts[3] - namely to treat patients effectively - these indicators seem to be a particular travesty, of little use to patients in trying to decide whether their illness would be better treated by Provider A or Provider B. But there is a further difficulty in any notion that ranking and star systems are intended to enhance the possibility of 'patient choice': whereas parents considering a choice of school for their child may well have time, resource, and clarity of mind to consider different options, many patients are in no such position; they are faced with the shock of illness, their lack of medical knowledge, and the urgent need to get something done quickly.

And of course, there is a further problem with all these 'choice-oriented' systems. This is the problem of equity in provision. If information is made available, and individuals are enabled to choose between alternatives, those who make the right choices will undoubtedly fare better. But what about those who make the wrong choices, or who are less well-informed? Or who find, having made a 'right choice', that the best places have all been taken up, and that they therefore have to settle for an inferior provider? It seems that any system of consumer choice will favour those with the capability, time and resources to make informed and determined choices - and penalise those who lack these. The government continues to proclaim its goal of ensuring, through its regulatory systems and increased expenditures, that minimum standards for all are maintained, and there is no reason to think that it is not successful in this - to a degree. But still, it seems likely that the outcome of a system designed to further consumer choice in public services will be an increase, not a decrease, in inequalities of provision within it.

There are bound to be as many individual losers as winners in systems of consumer choice, since at any given moment there can only be a limited number of superior options available. Thus, unless one accepts that greater inequality is desirable in itself, the case for a system of ranked and graded providers, operating

---

3. In a recent study, K. Rowan et al ('Hospital star ratings and clinical outcomes: ecological study', *British Medical Journal* (online) 23 January 04) reported that for adult critical care, the one field for which adequate data exist, star ratings do not reflect the quality of clinical care provided by hospitals: 'Patients do just as well in a trust with no stars as in one with three stars. Crude mortality data are misleading because they ignore the fact that higher rated trusts tend to be teaching institutions with patients who are less severely ill than on admission to critical care units.'

in competition with one another, depends on its success in raising average standards, in the medium or long run. Harm to losers in such systems (those who find themselves relying on providers labelled as inferior) might then be offset by the higher average standard brought about by enhanced competition. And 'special measures' are in any case taken to rescue the immediate casualties of failure, whilst the transfer of customers to better providers will also shift resources and give incentives to enhance performance. This is the justification for the effectiveness of competition and markets in general - good providers flourish and bad ones fail, and, on average and in the end, everyone benefits from the competition.

I s this argument valid for services where the vulnerability of consumers is large, and their difficulty in making informed choices great? This depends on whether these competitive mechanisms do have as their main effect the raising of standards in general, or whether they mainly widen the gaps between the standards of the more and less successful providers. But it seems likely that advantage and success are cumulative, with positive feedback effects as success becomes evident. The most capable staff are liable to move to the highest-regarded institutions, as do the most capable or advantaged consumers - which is no insignificant matter for the performance of a school or university. It may even be significant for a health provider, where oversubscription by needy and disadvantaged patients may have negative effects on its output standards. Far from reported failure stimulating greater effort, it may bring its own negative feedback, with loss of confidence, flight of clients and staff, and declining resources, all making it difficult to achieve 'turnarounds' from poor performance to good.

It seems certain that the commitment to ranking and competition is a part of an ideology which endorses structured inequalities in the quality of public service provision. The enhanced 'choice' that publics are held to demand includes opportunities to be superior and more privileged than others, not merely different from them. The enlarged middle class, who are the main electoral drivers of this priority, are individualist and competitive by ideological formation. Contradictory impulses on these questions struggle in the soul of the Labour Party, the goal of higher common standards contesting with that of enhancing opportunities to succeed in an unequal society. There seems little doubt about which side in this argument has been winning over recent decades. In so far as audit regimes provide measures and indicators of relative quality as one of their principal outputs, they serve the purposes of maintaining a system of unequal provision. (The current debate about variable funding for universities illuminates this implicit debate. Not long ago the regulatory system aimed to maintain a common standard for all universities, but the implications of current policy are that hierarchy between universities needs to be established and supported.)

Improving quality

The third potential objective of inspection and audit systems is for me the most interesting, though it is also the most neglected. This is the objective of improving quality and performance, not indirectly through the incentive or punitive effects of published rankings, indicators, or reports, but directly, through the learning that could take place during the interactions between inspectors and those they inspect, and in the preparations for and outcomes of inspections. How far is the experience of inspection and audit one which contributes *directly* to the enhancement of quality, and how far could it be expected, or indeed designed, to do this? One critical issue to consider here is whether this objective is consistent with the other two primary objectives identified above, or whether it is in competition with them, or indeed compromised by them. How far do choices have to be made between these different purposes, and the procedures, cultures and methodologies appropriate to them?

My experience as a member of staff groups who have been subject to inspections is that - although there is often acknowledged to have been some benefit from them in terms of improved practice - the gain is generally felt to be disappointingly small. The huge commitments required to meet the formal demands of inspections - the production of statements of purpose, the descriptions of procedures, the preparation of data, the planning of meetings, the establishment of adequate 'audit trails' - are often felt to bring a small return in what is learned during an inspection. Great anxiety is often followed by disillusionment, where inspection seems unable, through its protocols, to engage with the particulars of what it is looking at. Hopes that genuine dialogue or new insight will be provided by this process are too often dashed.

Some bad experiences of this kind are inevitable, and need not in themselves discredit the process. But I believe the problem to be more systemic than this, and that it is often manifest even when inspection teams are functioning reasonably well according to their procedures. The problem derives from the priority given in these systems to the first and the second of the objectives outlined above, as opposed to the third. Improving quality through interaction with those inspected simply isn't the main task of most inspection systems, nor the reason for which they were set up.

The two dominant objectives of most inspections - the assurance of acceptable common standards and establishing indicators to justify ranking by merit - have had a profound influence on the procedures they follow. Failure to meet standards can lead to sanction, while success or failure in the achievement of good rankings also brings reward or sanction. Because of this, criteria of fairness and probity have become central to the whole process, since in their absence, given the major implications of the results, those inspected and judged would claim that outcomes were ill-founded, biased, or unjust. To maintain fairness and probity, it is necessary that inspectors function according to standard procedures, following criteria for making assessments which are as objective and uniform as possible. Thus, although inspectors are normally drawn from the professional fields which are being inspected, their specific training as inspectors is in the procedures and criteria of evaluation - and not in the problems of assessing, still less of improving, the quality of work in their particular field.

The effect of this approach is to flatten out, and diminish in their importance, the differences between institutions and practices, since it is what they have in common which is of most relevance to auditors, not what is distinctive or unique about them. This tendency to standardisation has impacted significantly on the practices of institutions. For example, in higher education, it is required that the entire process of a course be described in writing, in a 'validated' course document which is given to students, and can be used by them to guide their own studies. These specifications are also seen as the 'terms and conditions of purchase' by students of the educational 'product', though it is doubtful if this consumerist conception is appropriate to educational provision.

In some ways this has been a beneficial process, bringing about a higher standard of preparation of syllabuses, reading lists and assessment requirements than might otherwise have been the case. But there has also been a tendency to homogenise and standardise not only the written description, but also the practice of a course, in order to meet regulatory requirements. Deviations from the norm are regarded as prospective problems, not as creative innovations. Furthermore, the norms of description which have evolved - no doubt for purposes of comparability, and to enable standard 'benchmarks' to be developed - have become removed from the way in which a sensible teacher might want to describe a course, or in which any sensible student might want to read about it. If every unit and every course has to be described in the same way as every other, it can almost be guaranteed than none of them will appear very interesting.

Indeed, a drive to homogenisation and standardisation of all procedures and practices seems endemic in these systems; it is part of the autopoietic production (as Niklas Luhmann calls it) of an institution's sovereignty over the processes which take place within its boundaries.[4] Inspection regimes invade the mentalities of the primary providers they regulate, as their demands are internalised, as well as responded to by calculation. Differences tend to be defined, a priori, as tending to unfairness. Why should some students have to write more essays than others, be taught for more weeks than others, have curriculum units of different sizes? I have sometimes felt that this process will only reach its conclusion when every university course in the UK, if not eventually the world, is identical in every respect except its specific subject content. It has become hard to sustain the view that difference can be a source of positive value.

This process is part of a larger context in which the demand for measurement is unduly influencing the practices that are being measured. Because core professional practices in education, health care or social services tend to be too complex, subtle and variable to be easily categorised, proxies for these practices are selected which do lend themselves to standard description and measurement. This means that, for instance, the frames placed over educational practices in universities to assess their quality filter out a great deal of the specific quality of learning interactions in the cause of producing reliable measures. The measuring of waiting lists, or time elapsed before appointments, is a comparable distortion in health care. Of course getting to see a doctor is a necessary condition of being treated successfully, but its

---

4. See Niklas Luhmann, *Risk: a Sociological Theory* (1993).

importance has to be balanced against an assessment of what happens once an appointment takes place, and how urgent the condition was in the first place. The latter is hard to measure, the former relatively easy, so this is what assessments have focused attention on. The question is whether such measures are assessing what is most important.

Since governments have instigated this process not only in order to improve these systems, but also to demonstrate to their electorates that they are improving them, a further distortion enters the picture, since appearances may, for the latter purpose, be what matter most.

Improving quality and organisational change

Improving quality self-evidently entails change. In organisations providing education, health and social care, achieving this is usually a complex and multi-dimensional affair. The 'national literacy hour' and additional stages of assessment were among the few 'quick fixes' that were ever available in this sphere. They were means of doing one or two 'big things', across a whole sector, that could probably make a difference. But most of the time it is difficult to get staff - as individuals or groups - or organisations to do things differently from the way they already do them. The more complex and differentiated a process of production, the more this is the case, and the less centralised systems of command and control will work.

One notices, for example, even in strong and effective organisations, how little transfer of good practice there seems to be between one specialism and another, even when managers understand that such transfers would be desirable. Staff have a relatively high degree of tenure in these fields, compared with others (this is in part a function of the value of their 'local knowledge' to their organisation); so it is hard to achieve improvements by the method of removing staff and appointing replacements. Work is often dependent on teams, and on their shared experience and understanding. Quality depends on ongoing relationships, including ongoing relationships with clients, pupils or patients. Changes are therefore likely to have beneficial effects, for good or ill, only after 'working through', and over a period of time. It is not surprising that, in the few empirical studies that have been made of quality of performance in such organisations (such as Michael Rutter et al's classic study of primary schools, *Fifteen Thousand*

Hours), leadership, staff morale, and organisational cohesion account for most of the variances in performance.[5]

These factors suggest that in these 'social' sectors there are likely to be serious problems in balancing the goals of achieving acceptable standards, establishing relative merits or rankings, and bringing about desirable changes. Each of these goals of inspection, and the activities associated with them, generates a different occupational culture and mentality.

For example, faced with prospective disgrace and sanction for falling below standard, organisations will conceal truths, and develop solidarity, even paranoia, towards the outside. This is not the state of mind in which deficiencies and limitations are readily thought about or admitted. The motivation for achieving high inspection scores, or avoiding low ones, may include more expansive attitudes than simple fear of failure, but the need to succeed will also encourage a concern for appearances over attention to reality. Such preoccupation with self-presentation is a feature of most of these inspection systems.

If the aim is to find out what could be improved in an organisation, and to think about how to bring improvements about, a different state of mind is called for. This requires, above all, trust - between colleagues, in organisational superiors, and in external inspectors who are having to bring bad as well as good news. Trust is needed because improvement is not possible without prior acknowledgement of weakness or deficiency (without this, why would improvement be necessary?); and no-one is going to explore their own deficiencies willingly if they believe they are going to be punished when these are discovered.

Of course this is the difficult situation in which teachers, therapists, organisational consultants - and indeed wise managers - find themselves, on a daily basis. They wish to bring about the equivalent of 'improvements in quality', in an individual or collective client's life or work. To do this they have to find a

---

5. The audit system has substantially taken the place of what should be independent social scientific investigation. Standardised measures - a poor quality, Fordist, kind of social science - substitute for inquiring and critical investigations of institutional practices (such as the Rutter study). The public resources devoted to the inspection system far exceeds the budget of the Economic and Social Research Council. The first head of Ofsted regarded most academic educational researchers, as well as the old HMIs, with contempt, and his agency developed a different method of investigating educational practice.

space in which weaknesses can be honestly contemplated, and in which the challenge and risk of doing something differently can be tolerated. This requires, above all, a non-judgemental attitude, an understanding that the consultant/ teacher/therapist has been there too, in some way or another, and a willingness to share at least some of the emotional burdens of the task. The process of improvement requires, in short, an identification with those with whom such work is taking place.

Thus, for teachers, perception and acknowledgement of what is not perfect in the learners has to be accompanied by respect and concern for the learners themselves. In practice, in educational contexts the functions of 'teaching' and 'assessment' are sometimes divided, with 'the exams' coming at the end of a teaching process, and even seeming to be the responsibility of a different entity ('the examiners') - though in practice these may include the same people. Some teachers may find it more comfortable to ally themselves with the students in their ordeal at the hands of a remote examining board, though this is a solution perhaps based on a reluctance to take on some of the responsibilities of the teacherly role. Nothing can be less like this 'learning relationship' than the usual connection between inspectors and inspected, which is brief in duration, impersonal in tone, and lacking in commitment to anything much, apart from probity and fairness in the discharge of the task. Often, inspectors and assessors are individuals who have themselves opted out of lasting institutional commitments, and are now working as part-time contractors. This situation may enhance their sense of detachment.

'no-one is going to explore their own deficiencies willingly if they believe they are going to be punished when these are discovered'

Reports by the HM Inspector of Prisons, however, suggest that they have a somewhat different approach, since these Reports sometimes refer back directly to earlier inspection visits, and attempt to evoke some shared common goals of improvement, as if to rally the energies of the staff in face of their difficult situation. The Prison Inspectorate Reports are also remarkably direct in their descriptions of the prison environment, and lack the filtering of reality through abstractions and protocols that characterises most of the other inspection formats. They are sometimes moving documents to read, which one would hardly say of most inspection reports. Reports by the HM Inspector of Prisons are based on a different approach. Tumim successfully campaigned for the abolition of the practice of 'slopping out'. Ramsbotham made the respect accorded to prisoners by staff a key measure of the quality of prison regimes. The Inspectorate of Prisons has sustained a position independent of government, while most of the others have been the enforcers of its 'modernising' agenda.

I am not wishing to argue that one of the three sets of objectives in audit and inspection - perhaps the 'softest' and most 'qualitative' - should be given priority over all the others. My case is rather that, unless we understand what these different objectives are, and how they compete and conflict with one another, we will never develop procedures and cultures which actually improve practice and the quality of services.

Different beliefs about motivation

These different perspectives on assessment - what one might call the sanctioning, competitive, and learning approaches - stem from different assumptions about human motivation and different conceptions of what is socially possible and desirable.[6] The sanctioning approach is committed above all to the necessity for compliance with obligations and standards. Those who advocated audit and inspection as a new regime of regulation did so because they were disillusioned with the main institutions that had previously been responsible for ensuring compliance, namely traditional bureaucracies. The quality of public services was supposed, traditionally, to be secured by compliance to law, by just and fair appointment processes, and by the existence of ordered hierarchies in government services. Subsequently it was argued that these systems no longer functioned effectively, that they had been 'captured' by their employees, etc. However, the new regulatory systems designed to 'modernise' the old in fact operate with similar motivational assumptions. Instead of direct regulation and control, through bureaucratic hierarchies, there is now indirect regulation and

---

6. These different inspection practices map on to Amitai Etzioni's three models of compliance set out in *A Comparative Analysis of Complex Organisations* (1961). Etzioni distinguishes between mainly coercive institutions, institutions which function chiefly through material rewards, and institutions which rely on moral consensus and solidarity for their cohesion.

control, through quasi-independent agencies which nevertheless act with the force and power of law. The indirectness of this form of governance has enabled government to exercise huge power, whilst escaping direct political accountability for it. Indeed it is made to appear that the real power lies in impersonal systems and criteria, and not in human agents at all. This system has reproduced in its turn the defects of the earlier compliance-oriented systems it was intended to replace, namely pseudo-compliance, alienation of staff, and rigidity and ritualism in task-performance.

Competitive approaches to inspection, via rankings and merit stars, seek to mobilise the desire for reward, power and prestige, rather than merely the desire to avoid disgrace and failure. They do undoubtedly mobilise competitive efforts, and may galvanise mechanisms for improvement and learning within competing organisations. As already noted, there is little evidence about the effects of these systems, one way or another. But it would be interesting to learn whether the competitive pressures brought about by these systems have in fact led to development within them, and to changes in their relative success, or whether they have merely reproduced existing differences in resource and capability. The evidence of the universities is that the entrenchment of performance scores and league tables as a result of audit systems has frozen the pre-existing institutional hierarchy. This is hardly a surprising outcome given that the government is so committed to inequalities - termed 'excellence' - in this and other public spheres. Both the 'sanction' and 'competitive' models of regulation are essentially individualist and interest-oriented, rather than solidaristic and value-oriented.

The 'learning model' makes different assumptions about productive motivations, believing in relationship, trust, and co-operation as the preconditions for development, not only within institutions, but also in their transactions with external authorities. David Marquand elaborated these differences of philosophical view in *The Unprincipled Society* (1988), where he advocated the idea of a society committed to learning - differences between philosophical individualism, and the tradition usually thought of as idealist. This latter tradition now has few advocates in Britain. New Labour's commitment to 'modernise' the public services is largely constructed on individualist assumptions, continuous with those of the previous Conservative governments, though more inclusive if not more egalitarian in aim. What remains absent from, indeed disliked by, New Labour, is an alternative conception of 'the public' and 'the social' as representing a different kind of solidarity and commitment. These ideas are viscerally regarded as a mere ideological masquerade for the self-interest of public sector professions and unions.

It was no accident that the first chief Inspector of OFSTED, Chris Woodhead, designer of the original template for public sector inspection systems, remained in office for three years after New Labour came to office. He was both hostile to teachers and committed to methods of inspection that depended on sanction and competition as their primary motivational levers. Yet the type of regime of audit and inspection he instituted now provides the 'micro-structure' of regulation of our increasingly individualised, though also heavily governed society. It is one of its distinctive regimes of power. (The Foucauldian tradition in social theory provides many useful concepts for analysing such regimes.)

An alternative system of inspection and audit?

It is possible, I believe, to devise a method of audit and inspection that is committed to the achievement of common agreed standards, in each sphere of public provision, but is also committed to shared learning and the improvement of practice. But it is doubtful whether these objectives could be combined with the other major goal of current audit systems - the generation of evidence on which competitive rankings can be based. It would be possible, however, to achieve a consensus about what basic standards should be - even about desirable improvements in these over time - that would not divide the inspected from inspectors. (Those whose offences are tried in courts of law are not usually divided from their judges by profoundly different conceptions of right and wrong, but rather by different views of their own particular circumstances and deserts.) Indeed, one can envisage that the first task of any audit and inspection system would be to establish, through quantitative and qualitative indicators, where an institution or agency stands in regard to these accepted norms - perhaps taking into account its particular situation regarding location, clientele, etc - and then to make recommendations for remedy and improvement which would have the force of obligation.

But once that threshold of adequacy has been achieved, a different role becomes appropriate for systems of inspection. This is to clarify what is distinctive and particular about the goals of an agency or institution, by requiring it to formulate these, and to identify criteria for their evaluation and assessment. A presupposition of this process would be that agencies in these fields are inherently different from one another, and that such differences can be a source of value. The government has to some degree moved towards such an acknowledgement in its advocacy of 'specialist schools', and even 'foundation hospitals' - though it is clear that other purposes, favouring not only difference but also enhanced stratification and ranking, are mixed up with this.

In the kind of regime I am describing, inspectors would be required to consider specifications of purpose, and to report on achievements in relation to these, in ways which took account of their particularity. Measures of assessment that were appropriate and relevant to some agencies would not be so relevant to others. Audits would be required first to report on how far institutions met basic objectives. But they would then go on to report on how well they were doing on other criteria, partly identified by the agency concerned, and partly from the pool of relevant knowledge and criteria which inspectors would bring to their task.

In particular, agencies would be expected to demonstrate their commitment and capacity for improvement, against the criteria they agree with inspectors, and the task of inspection would be in part to explore their success or difficulties with this process. One of the purposes of inspectors would be, in consultancy or facilitation mode, to assist and catalyse this process, from their own knowledge and experience. This might require an insistence that different elements of an institution are brought together, that acknowledged or discovered problems are discussed and analysed, and that follow-up reports are submitted on progress achieved. This would become a much more open-ended and thus variable process, but it might also be one that was more vital and productive.

Compliance is in any case not much use as a habit of mind in a competitive world in which innovation is necessary to create value. A process of inspection and audit which encourages innovation and discovery might, one would hope, have some effects 'all the way down', on the habits of managements, staff, and pupils and clients themselves. Our present systems of regulation by contrast encourage standardisation, defensive self-presentation, and risk-avoidance, and this goes all the way down too.

Among the inspectors in such a system there would need to be capable innovators and facilitators, whose satisfaction and reputation would come from success in influencing and catalysing good practice. It does not seem to me that many people now join inspection services because they believe that this is going to be their best opportunity to bring about innovations, though this was the case at an earlier stage in an organisation like the ILEA, where educational developments were initiated and guided through its advisory services. Such an approach would also have an implication for what institutions would themselves need to do to work successfully in this environment. Instead of the risk-avoiders and compliance-specialists for which the present system now selects, one would hope to see 'quality innovators' and 'quality entrepreneurs' become the key figures in these processes - as developers of new programmes became in the early days of the new universities. Indeed the presence of individuals taking such roles would be a sign of health in such institutions.

M uch stress is now laid by government on responsiveness to customers and customer-satisfaction as criteria of good practice and good governance. It would be possible for an inspection system to be oriented towards 'consumer involvement' if the reports on which it was based, and the rituals of discussion and reflection which it generated, were made accessible to publics, especially to the local communities which provide the clients for a service. I don't think one could read an average OFSTED Report and imagine that it would form a lively basis for a public institutional review. But one could imagine the design of a different kind of reporting document, intended to be read by all members and associates of an agency as well as by inspectors, which could form the basic text for 'hearings' to be held in public. This might take the form of a Report by an institution to its members and clients, which an inspecting body, as part of its remit, would question and discuss. The inspectors' own report would subsequently make a further contribution to this assessment, which in any case would have to include genuine self-assessment to be productive.

There has to be some tension in such proceedings for them to have value and authenticity; the confrontation between those submitting a report and inspectors would thus necessarily include elements of uncertainty and potential for conflict. It would indeed be this potential for difficulty, and its experience from time to time, which would signify that this democratic process was a genuine one. Skills and roles would need to be developed for the operation of a system oriented towards self-reflection and improvement, but this would be of benefit in itself. Indeed it is hard to see that 'user involvement' in public services will ever amount to much unless procedures and practices which make possible the exercise of 'voice' and 'loyalty', in Albert Hirschman's terms, as well as customer 'exit' are brought into being.

Conclusion

It is not my purpose to argue against the principle or practice of the accountability of public services and public institutions; nor am I asking for inspectors to 'go away and leave us alone', though it is perhaps understandable that many professionals do react in this way, in response to what they see as the oppressiveness and mindlessness of their regulatory regimes.

On the contrary, I am in favour of a lively system of audit and inspection, but one which has as one of its principal goals to stimulate, facilitate, and support ongoing improvements in practice. I think this goal is consistent with that of improving common standards. Once these basic aims are met, the work of improvement and innovation can begin, within a different culture and practice. I don't think that such a system can also be used to provide data to effect the competitive ranking of public providers without damage to its quality-enhancing function. Of course, informal and formal rankings will be made anyway, by a host of people and media. But just as organisational consultants do not go around marking their clients out of ten, and publishing their marks, so must institutional auditors maintain a distance between their work and such competitive measurement. They should seek instead to promote self-understanding and change among their clients, and, through publication and circulation, in the wider community.

Systems of inspection and accountability could become a form of democratic empowerment, encouraging collective identification with the public sphere. New means of citizens' involvement are urgently needed to revitalise democratic practices, which are currently being eroded by the 'mediatisation' of politics, and by the decline of political parties as communities of conviction.

The present government proclaims a commitment to improve and 'modernise' public services, and has belatedly increased investment in them. But it does not seem to have a conception of what is distinctively 'public' about a public service, except that its users do not pay for it at the point of use. Its dominant concept of 'modernisation' is based on the same assumptions about individual self-interest and the necessity for market competition as those that prevail in the market sector. The micro-regime of regulation developed in recent years has been in part the instrument of this conception. This article suggests an alternative view, one which gives predominant emphasis to co-operation and trust, and to the common pursuit of improvement.

Comments on this article will be welcome at m.j.rustin@uel.ac.uk

A version of this article was first presented at a Tavistock Clinic Policy Seminar in October 2003.

The Blairlusconi phenomenon

Geoff Andrews

Geoff Andrews *sees some disquieting parallels between Blair and Berlusconi.*

I have spent the last three years researching and writing about Silvio Berlusconi. It has been an extraordinary time, watching Italy's richest man extend his power and influence over 90 per cent of Italian TV, passing legislation to make himself immune from prosecution for corruption, increasing his financial empire, and openly rounding on 'communist' magistrates who have made attempts to bring him to court.

His postmodern populism has ensured that his frequent public gaffes as a statesman have been met with indifference by many of his fellow citizens - who continue to view him as a salesman, and hope that his entrepreneurialism will bring them wealth and prosperity. Yet this populism is symptomatic of an arrogance of power; and it also undermines public trust, and devalues the importance of politics and democracy. It has enabled Berlusconi to preside over the decline of Italy's body politic, to become the most degenerate in Western Europe.

The unprecedented concentration of his power allows open rein to his contempt for opposition and dissent. Berlusconi's critics, including several well-known comedians, have been taken off the air of RAI, the state broadcaster. Meanwhile Berlusconi himself has distributed writs against anyone who has questioned his intentions. *The Economist* magazine has been in frequent communication with his lawyers after claiming he was 'unfit to govern'. Dario Fo, the playwright and comedian, himself a recipient of a writ for defamation for his latest play - where he prances around the stage as a deranged Berlusconi

- has said his show was a last resort: 'We could not just sit by the window and watch Berlusconi go by. We had to do something'.

While one half of Italy has remained largely indifferent to Berlusconi's shenanigans, the other half looks on with a mixture of horror and ridicule. 'You're lucky', Italian friends have said to me. 'You still have a free press. Your Prime Minister doesn't own or control the media'. As the Berlusconi and Blair eras started to unravel, however, and as I travel backwards and forwards on low-cost airlines, the lines which previously divided Blair and Berlusconi have started to get blurred. The crisis of public life so apparent in Italy is also becoming more evident, for different reasons, back home.

Blair of course is not in the same position as Berlusconi, whose concentration of ownership and power is unique in the modern era. Yet, he is constantly in thrall to the Murdoch press. One could easily be under the impression that Blair and his advisers see their entire future as dependent on support from Murdoch's populist newspapers. My friends in Italy have started to revise their earlier opinion. They were surprised at Blair's alliance with Berlusconi on the need for flexible labour markets, an issue which led to massive demonstrations in Italy. They were shocked at the spectacle of Blair cajoling Berlusconi and his 'post-fascist' allies into stronger backing for the US position on the Iraq War ('Thanks Silvio. You are a credit to your country'). And by the time that Blair commended Berlusconi in the House of Commons in December 2003 for his 'great skill and tenacity' in leading the Italian Presidency of the European Union - an incumbency seen by everyone else as an unmitigated disaster - their surprise had turned to despair.

Yet it is not only Blair's political links with Berlusconi that are a cause for concern. The aftermath of the Hutton inquiry has revealed a malaise in British public life that mirrors in important ways the Italian situation. The Blair government's response to the Hutton inquiry cannot be seen as merely an intemperate backlash. It is indicative of the managerial populism which now defines their mode of governance. Where for Berlusconi it is the magistrates and the unions that get in the way, for Blair it is the intellectuals and public servants. In both cases, delivery and efficiency are paramount. Winning is the only option. Independence of thought, dissent, and free journalistic expression which cannot be controlled, are seen as troublesome.

True, Alastair Campbell's bullying interventions never went as far as those of Maurizio Gasparri, Italy's post-fascist Minister for Communications, who once angrily rang RAI live on air to complain of political bias. But as an unelected official in a role previously confined to civil servants, Campbell was instrumental in making control freakery and corporate loyalty the modus operandi of government. According to Greg Dyke in his resignation comments, Campbell kept up a barrage of complaints against the BBC during the war, which amounted to a 'rant' in the eyes of senior BBC executives. It is easy to understand the view that Campbell's triumphalism at the Hutton verdict was derived from a relentless determination to make sure the BBC got a good kicking.

It is quite clear that the issues raised by Hutton will not be resolved by a few conciliatory words by Blair, who hopes that it 'will allow us to draw a line and move on'; nor is the situation likely to be helped by the moral sermonising of Peter Mandelson, a man who irresistibly calls to mind a slick Italian politician who can't stay away from the corridors of power, yet is now calling for a renewal of public trust.

For one thing, the person responsible for appointing the successor to Greg Dyke is Tessa Jowell, the Culture Secretary. Jowell has already pre-empted the Hutton report to some extent - in her strong criticisms of the BBC, and arguments that reform is long overdue. It is some irony, of course, that Jowell's husband David Mills has acted as a media lawyer for Berlusconi over a long period of time - as late as March 2003 Mills gave evidence in Berlusconi's defence against corruption charges. And as a company secretary of one of Berlusconi's businesses, Mills helped him purchase Italian media rights in the formative stages of his career as a media entrepreneur, as he embarked on his long-standing conflict with RAI. Presumably Ms Jowell won't be short of advice when it comes to dealing with 'obstructive' public service journalists.

The resignations of the heads of the BBC resemble those at RAI, after Berlusconi filled the board with political appointees. Indeed, anyone wanting to foresee the result of further government interference in the work of the BBC should look at the dangerous precedent in Italy, where Lucia Annunziata, President of the Board of RAI, recently resigned, arguing that the 'Gasparri Law' - the latest attempt to reform RAI along market lines - would further erode its independence. President Ciampi, disturbed by what he sees as the further centralisation of power, has refused to sign this new bill into law. The crisis this precipitated is ongoing, and has initiated one of Italy's biggest constitutional conflicts.

The situation in Britain is not identical to Italy. However, the BBC, like RAI, is facing the biggest crisis in its history. More significantly, Blair and Berlusconi share a form of governance which thrives on a weak opposition, low-trust societies, political disengagement and media populism. In the Berlusconi scenario, his ownership of three TV channels has been matched by the ability to manipulate to his own ends the state broadcaster. For Blair, it is the relationship with Murdoch and the certainties of managerialism that have undermined the conventions of politics.

For Italy and the UK, the consequences of the broadcasting crises for dissent and the health of public life are very serious. The respective crises have helped draw new faultlines over the future of politics, lines which are likely to outlast their own governments. The campaign by prominent BBC personalities and the walkouts by its staff resembled the protests against Berlusconi in Italy, led by the film director Nanni Moretti. The sight of BBC employees marching out in support of Greg Dyke, and cars honking their horns, seem more redolent of a Roman piazza than White City.

Silvio Berlusconi and Tony Blair promised much - an economic 'miracle' of low taxes and prosperity in the first case, a modern 'trust-based' society which would 'lead in Europe' in the second. Both can now be seen as absurd claims. More likely, their lasting legacies will be the corrosion of public institutions, the centralisation of power and the proliferation of cynicism and distrust amongst the public.

Pakistan at a crossroads

Sayeed Hasan Khan

Sayeed Khan *looks at the history of relations between Pakistan, India and Afghanistan, and detects some hope for progress in Kashmir.*

The history of decolonisation and partition still has profound effects on contemporary political life in Pakistan. Since 1948 there have been many disputes between Pakistan and India, not least over Kashmir, and there have also been many problems with Afghanistan. This has created a sense of vulnerability in successive Pakistani regimes. This needs to be understood in looking at current relations between the three countries.

Furthermore, the Muslim League in Pakistan in some senses came to power after independence without having gone through all the highly instructive troubles of a long, wrenching, and full-scale freedom struggle. The League had evolved not so much as an anti-colonial force, but more as a movement against the Congress Party, with its main aim being to carve out a state for the Muslims. This they were successful in winning, though in an unspeakably gory partition. Because of this history, Pakistanis today still use the word partition almost as a synonym when they think, write or talk of independence. And this lack of struggle against the British has shaped post-independence history in a number of ways, including the structures of government that were set up in 1948.

At the moment of independence Pakistan inherited an army and a bureaucracy which, though native, were thoroughly steeped in the haughty colonial styles of their departing British masters. Pakistan was also saddled with the Durand line as the boundary between Afghanistan and Pakistan (the line was named after the English official who crudely and arbitrarily drew it up), which the British had bullied the Afghans into accepting. The Durand line divided the large population of Pashto-speaking Pakhtuns between the two nations, and was to vex relations between the two countries ever afterward. Furthermore, when the British left, Pakistan continued to rule the Pakhtun region that remained within Pakistan with the same unimaginative bureaucrats who had ruled on behalf of the Viceroy; and these bureaucrats also continued in their colonial predecessors' arrogant attitude towards their Afghan neighbours - though without the imperial muscle. This galling treatment resulted in the Afghans cosying up to Pakistan's old enemy, India.

The only area of modern Pakistan where a significant anti-British movement had arisen before independence (a movement which had links with Nehru and Gandhi) was the North West Frontier Province, which is on the border with Afghanistan. After independence, the region's Pakhtun nationalist elite remained very friendly towards Kabul (their leader, Ghaffar Khan - known as the Frontier Gandhi - spent his eventual exile in Afghanistan, and is now buried there). Thus, from the start, Pakistan state authorities felt sandwiched between two hostile countries, and this view, justified or not, has over-ridden and distorted its foreign and domestic policies. Given such a keen sense of vulnerability, there was also little chance that the authorities would take a conciliatory line on the interminable Kashmir dispute.

Pakistan's best chance for transforming this weak geopolitical situation came after the Soviet invasion of Afghanistan in 1979, when the USA decided to utilise Pakistan, then under the leadership of General Zia, as a convenient conduit for western aid to the Mujahidin resistance. So General Zia's regime, with the hearty co-operation of CIA and the British, happily took control of the direction of the war in Afghanistan, channelling resources into the hands of its favoured fighters, in the meantime siphoning off plenty of side payments for itself. The now notorious intelligence unit of the Pakistan army, ISI, played a key role in Afghanistan - and it also was used by Zia to suppress domestic opposition, thus helping him to consolidate his dictatorship. Also during this period, the madrassas (religious schools), which had already existed for a long time in both Afghanistan and Pakistan, began to engage in training jihadis, the so-called holy warriors. It was only after the West began courting and mobilising the mullahs for the guerrilla war against the USSR that militancy among the students of these madrassas ignited and spread. Thus, Western democracies, with amazing alacrity and short-sightedness, stoked the jihadis' holy war, not knowing or even caring where it would all stop. This barely covert activity ultimately resulted in a takeover of the Kabul regime by the Taliban, the storm trooper students of the madrassas. Furthermore, before the Taliban took power, all the local warlords had been encouraged to increase opium and heroin production to finance the war. Thus it came about that the period of Taliban rule was the only time during the whole of the last fifty years that the Pakistani authorities felt comfortable in Kabul - though perhaps they were slow to realise that Pakistani society was also becoming Talibanised. It suited Pakistan leaders to have the Taliban as allies, and to regulate them through the flow of arms.

The war against the Soviets in Afghanistan thus not only boosted fundamentalist ambitions but also inundated Pakistan with narcotics. General Zia also cynically used the Islamic card to shore up his wobbly rule. To this end he resurrected the *hudood* ordinance, which imposed severe medieval-style punishments for consuming alcohol, fornication, property theft and other infractions. Women were the main victims of Zia's disingenuous Islamisation agenda. When these ordinances began, in 1979, there were 70 women in prison; when Zia died in a plane crash in 1988 the number had soared to 6000. Although the prosecution of cases under the Zina ordinance (forbidding fornication) has now dropped off, thousands of women are still in prison: once repressive laws are on the books, politicians are usually reluctant to repeal them.

The blasphemy law causes most suffering to minorities. If an unscrupulous Muslim has a property dispute with a non-Muslim, it makes things easier if they accuse the Christian or Hindu opponent of blasphemy, and the corrupt police are always ready to oblige. What's more, the Saudi financing of Pakistan's madrassas, though longstanding, has increased massively in recent years, as has fanatical Wahabi sectarianism. This has always been a problem for Pakistan's Shia Muslim population, and the dire Wahabi influence has sparked a spate of killings of Shia professionals. In the last three years over seventy Shia doctors have been murdered, and dozens of doctors and other Shia professionals have emigrated as a result of this persecution. All this in turn has led to a worsening in Pakistan's relations with neighbouring Iran, a Shia state.

Apart from narcotics and fundamentalism, the weapons overspill of the Afghan war has also introduced the ferocious 'Kalashnikov culture', which has brought about a deterioration in law and order throughout the country. The ruling class, backed by the army through its intelligence wing, has simply exploited all these miserable conditions for their own benefit. Each of the main political parties - the People's Party led by Benazir Bhutto, and the Muslim League of Nawaz Sharif (who was ousted from office by Musharraf) - has robbed the state and used Islamic forces against the left, which had tried to stand up for the rights of women, the poor and the minorities. Each of these dubiously democratic party's governments has also been terminated by army coups - General Musharraf's seizing of power in 1999 being the most recent. This coup occurred at a time when Pakistan had just been involved in a costly mini-war ('Kargil') against India, and was enduring increasingly bad relations with Iran; it also coincided with the peak of the havoc being wrought by the Taliban fanatics it had nurtured in Kabul. For a while the army takeover made Pakistan a pariah state, until in 2001 9\11 restored the wisely accommodating army regime to favour - they knew an offer they could not refuse when the vengeful US made them one.

The Musharraf regime

After 9/11, the Musharraf regime ruthlessly cut loose the Taliban, gutted and reorganised the ISI, and leant support to the Western assault on Afghanistan. Still Pakistan was not quite off the hook, however: India persuaded the Western powers that Pakistan was aiding the cross-border movement of terrorists into Kashmir. This was indeed the case, as many holy warriors who had fought against the Soviets were now idle, and were eager to join the insurgency in the valley; and, since, after two bad maulings in wars over Kashmir, the Pakistan army did not have the stomach to engage in another duel itself, the ISI had come to rely on fervent mujahidins to bleed the Indian side. But as, post-9/11, the Americans were not prepared to tolerate fundamentalists anywhere any more, they pressured Musharraf to withdraw support from these zealots and stop their raids and activities in Indian-held Kashmir. (This inflow of fanatical elements had also altered the complexion of the liberation struggle of Kashmir, which until then had been totally secular in character. The jihadis also alienated the sizeable group of Muslims in the Indian part of Kashmir.) Musharraf went along with Bush on Afghanistan, but was reluctant to go against all the fundamentalist organisations whose support had been so useful; he was unable to resist American pressure, however, and decided to rein these forces in, though they had been the 'B team' of the army for so long.

This is why there has been a fresh breeze blowing lately not only inside Pakistan but also across the border. Indian prime minister and BJP leader Vajpayee has now met with Musharraf, after previously refusing to see him. For his part Musharraf made the bold announcement that he was prepared to set aside the UN resolutions on Kashmir - which used to be the obstructive mantra of every Pakistani leader. Helping the cause of conciliation was the fact that there were no mass demonstrations against Vajpayee - not even by religious groups - when he attended the SAARC (South Asia Association for Regional Co-operation) conference in Islamabad early in 2004. The Pakistan-India People's Forum for Peace and Democracy, which has been meeting in various cities of the subcontinent over the last ten years, also met in Karachi at around the same time as the SAARC meeting: three hundred Indian professionals travelled to Pakistan to discuss with their fellow delegates from Pakistan the prospects for, and the road to, peace between the two nuclear powers. Ashok Mitra, a noted Marxist economist from India, participated in the Forum, as did many media and film personalities.

Road, air and train links have also reopened - always a key indicator of national tempers - and there are promises of further improvements in the relations between the two countries. Ultimately, Pakistan will have to relinquish claims on the Indian part of Kashmir, while the Indians will have to genuinely meet the demands of local insurgents who want their rights restored. Pakistan must come to terms with the real ethnic and creedal complexities of Kashmir: in the Indian areas the valley is predominantly Muslim, but Ladakh and Jammu have Buddhist and Hindu majorities, though with a good chunk of Muslims too. Since independence India and Pakistan have both treated Kashmir as if it were merely a disputed piece of property, with no residents living there. It is possible that in the new atmosphere Kashmiris finally may get a chance to be treated as human beings, and the killing and injustices will be stopped.

When Musharraf, under strong Western pressure, ordered elections in 2002, the fundamentalists were the only group contesting the elections who were opposed to the American invasion of Afghanistan. Ironically, the election enabled these quarrelling fundamentalist groups to unite for the first time around a single platform, and to win majorities in two of the four provinces of the country. They suddenly became the main opposition in the national parliament, whereas previously they had in general only managed to win a dozen seats between them. As well as their new unity, their success was due to their anti-imperialist stance, at a time when all the other parties were visibly cowed by American power. (The more secular left was too insignificant to take advantage of widespread anti-imperial apprehensions.) At the end of 2003 - through judicial use of the stick and the carrot - Musharraf succeeded in securing support for a constitutional agreement which enabled him to legitimise himself: he was elected president by the majority of the national and provincial assembly members. MMA - the six-party fundamentalist alliance - is currently co-operating with the regime. However, it is clear that Musharraf is still facing danger at the hand of extremists; and he has recently survived two attempts on his life. Given this extremist spectre, there is a widespread feeling among the various sectors of Pakistani society that peace with India is vital for Musharraf, in spite of his evasiveness regarding a restoration of domestic political life. The West very much wants to keep him in power, for his help in Afghanistan and in the control of local fanatical threats. Domestically the country may not have benefited much from the rule of Musharraf, either economically or administratively, but if he succeeds in soothing relations with India his rule will have contributed a major achievement. At the moment he seems to be the only authority in Pakistan who can accomplish this worthwhile goal - provided he is safe from a determined Osama.

Celebrity and 'meritocracy'

Jo Littler

In our contemporary meritocratic culture, new possibilities of social and cultural transition are being produced alongside sharp inequalities of wealth and status. Jo Littler examines the ways in which current forms of celebrity culture reflect - and produce - this state of affairs, and considers why celebrity is a political issue.

You better lose yourself in the music, the moment
You own it, you better never let it go
You only get one shot, do not miss your chance to blow
This opportunity comes once in a lifetime yo.[1]

In the lyrics to Eminem's *Lose Yourself*, fame is not simply something that anyone talented can get if they work hard enough. The moments when it might pay off to strive are few and far between: celebrity is a chance moment, a fleeting conjunction, something necessary to seize because of its rarity. You mess up the moment and you will be back in the place you came from, the place to which you do not wish to return. Fame here is not the inevitable outcome of the diligent buffing up of some 'raw talent'. Nor is it the low-risk Protestant celebrity work ethic offered by *Fame Academy*. Eminem's lyrics describe a society in which

---

1. The full lyrics from this and other songs quoted in this article can be found at a range of online lyric sites such as http://www.azlyrics.com/c.html.

celebrity is more a random - and potentially cruel - lottery than a birthright for the righteously dedicated. They figure the fragility of fame, and articulate a sense of slim pickings, a place in which there are not many chances - a world in which it is thus all the more important to recognise any chances that occur, and channel intense energy into taking them up. In part the intensity comes from this sense that it is as easy to lose everything as it is difficult to gain it.

*L*ose Yourself zooms in upon and dramatises this moment of chance. As in 8 Mile, the film to which these lyrics are soundtrack (and whose hero 'Rabbit' is a semi-fictionalised representation of Eminem, the celebrity who plays him), the possibilities of becoming famous are depicted amidst a deprived social backdrop, about which a complex tangle of sentiments and messages are expressed. 8 Mile is a powerful indictment of the injustice of American poverty, bringing to the big screen images of the depressed urban detritus of downsized industrialisation, and dramatising with eloquent rage the difficulties of those kicked to the bottom of the social pile. At the same time, its implied solution is the individualistic achievement of pulling yourself up by the bootstraps against the odds (an ethos leading some commentators to describe Eminem as 'the President's friend' - see Johann Hari, *Independent on Sunday*, 12.1.03). There are other ambivalences too. The masculinity of our hero is reconfigured enough to promote a model of caring sensitivity towards children, yet not enough to have reworked its misogyny (all adult women are both inappropriately sexual and let him down badly). The film presents its hybrid social groupings with easy familiarity, endorses an anti-essential understanding of 'race', is alive to some of racism's effects and shows itself to be aware of the issue of appropriating cultures. Yet at the same time the relationship between the white hero and black cultures remains one in which 'cool' is co-opted, and through which authenticity is sought and garnered; and it is a relationship from within which the hero ultimately emerges as triumphant, implicitly leaving it behind.

If 8 Mile and Lose Yourself explicitly and expressively grapple with a range of contemporary topics and issues, they also display an array of motifs characteristic of our present mode of celebrity culture, motifs which are, in turn, related to these issues around 'race', gender and inequalities of opportunity. Firstly, they invite us to get very intimate with the emotions of a celebrity: the slippery flux and continuum of Eminem's star persona is heavily dependent on the appearance of him authentically mining and exposing the details of his life. Secondly, both film and song are highly reflexive about the business of being a celebrity, offering commentaries on some of the 'rules' of the game. And thirdly, they focus on the moment just *before* becoming famous: presenting this moment of graft, of striving, of desire, as a moment of raw 'realness', of authenticity. These three themes - 'real' pre-fame, intimacy and reflexivity - have an entrenched cultural currency beyond this specific instance. All three themes contribute to generating the desire for fame and at the same time making it seem 'ordinary'.

Celebrity, media power and meritocracy

One of the most useful ways to begin to think about current forms of celebrity culture, and its relationship to wider shifts in the dynamics of social and cultural power, is to draw on Nick Couldry's work on media power and its relation to 'the ordinary'. Couldry writes that:

> By 'media power', I do not mean the power (ideological or otherwise) exercised upon us by specific media texts; I mean more generally media institutions' differential symbolic power, the concentration of symbolic power in media institutions: that is, the fact that we take it for granted that the media have the power to speak 'for us all' - indeed to define the social 'reality' that we share - a power which individuals, corporations, pressure groups, professional bodies and even perhaps the state do not have.[2]

Couldry draws from Bourdieu, from Sennett and Cobb's theories of the hidden injuries of class, and from his own interviews with 'ordinary' people, to argue that there is a constructed symbolic boundary between 'the media world' and 'the ordinary world'. He argues that the 'media world' is marked as a symbolic space of authority, while 'the ordinary world' is a space marked by its lack of validation. It is in the gap between these worlds that the 'hidden injuries of media power' are formed. This gives us some very useful tools with which to think about the hidden injuries of celebrity as well as media power, and Couldry does point us in this direction, arguing that programmes like *Big Brother*, in which

---

2. Nick Couldry, 'The hidden injuries of media power' in *Journal of Consumer Culture*, Vol 1 No 2 November 2001 pp155-177. See also his *The Place of Media Power: Pilgrims and Witnesses of the Media Age*, Routledge 2000.

'ordinary' people become celebrities, do not so much transcend the division between worlds as work to reinscribe it. 'To put it crudely', he writes, 'why else would the transition to celebrity (and the games played in celebrity's border zones) matter so much?' (p172). In these terms, media celebrity becomes a means of symbolic validation, a way to 'really' exist, to mean something in public and private, to be rich with symbolic as well as material capital. To seek the full glare of celebrity media validation is to strive against the hidden injuries of disempowerment; to strive against the symbolic disempowerment of the 'ordinary'.

Of course we are not particularly used to thinking of not-being-a-celebrity in the potentially hyperbolic and victimised terms of 'an injury'. But Couldry's schema is extremely useful as it names a phenomenon and a scale that has different levels of intensity. Viewed in this way, it resonates with other academic and critical understandings of the relationship between celebrity, media and society. Thus (as David Morley summarises Suzanne Moore), talk shows can demonstrate 'the simple but powerful capacity of the media to offer these participants some form of recognition, however perverse, of their existence'.[3] And the importance of such recognition is not something only felt by these few; as Chris Rojek writes:

> To some extent, the dynamics of modern society mean that all of us are caught up in the celebrity race. It is axiomatic that only a minority acquire the public acclaim and recognition that we associate with celebrity status. It is also axiomatic that if the majority suffer from feelings of rejection and invalidation, they internalize them in ways that pose no threat to the social order.[4]

In other words, what Rojek calls rejection and invalidation, what Moore/Morley might term a lack of recognition, and what Couldry calls 'injuries', have a lot in common. Whether at the extreme or 'normal' end of the spectrum, these strategies of cultural coping or non-coping indicate a society and a culture that has developed some extraordinarily unequal ways to validate people's sense of

---

3. David Morley, *Home Territories: Media, Mobility and Identity*, Routledge 2000 p111.
4. Chris Rojek, *Celebrity*, Reaktion Books 2001, p147.

self and collective worth.

Whilst celebrity culture can be understood in terms of symbolic disempowerment, it can also be understood in the context of economic and social disempowerment: in terms of unequal access to material resources and social mobility. Here we need to consider the character of the political conjuncture we inhabit in terms of the Blairite vision of Britain as a meritocracy. A meritocracy is nowadays understood as 'a social system which allows people to achieve success proportionate to their talents and abilities, as opposed to one in which social class or wealth is the controlling factor'.[5] This is part of the wider frame of post-fordist late capitalism, in which relatively rigid class identity distinctions have to some extent fractured and multiplied. Whilst the routes between class stratifications have become marginally more porous - generating some high profile examples - substantial class mobility remains out of reach for the majority. And divisions of wealth have become greatly exacerbated over the last few decades.

Crucially, the Blairite vision is not of an equality of wealth (as under 'old' Labour), but rather of a state that facilitates the ability to strive for it. As with the logic of late capitalism more broadly, this implicitly rests on the proposition that it is only possible for a few people to be really 'successful'. At the same time, however, the structural drive of Blairite policies - as with other neo-liberal governments - has been to increase marketised competition and to further the dismantling of the welfare state, resulting in the destruction of collective provision and the erosion of provision for the poor. This has exacerbated the inequalities of opportunity from which 'talent' (in itself a problematic enough concept) can be healthy enough, culturally equipped enough, or even well fed enough, to 'rise' through the cultural and social pool. In other words, even taken within its own terms, this discourse of meritocracy fails. That people do not surface at the top through 'merit' alone is flamboyantly illustrated in the US context by the nepotistic career of the current president. As the supportive structures of social welfare institutions become impoverished,

---

5. Michael Young coined the word 'meritocracy' in his book, *The Rise of the Meritocracy 1870-2033*, Penguin, 1958. He later claimed Blair was woefully misusing it. See Michael Quinion's article on his website *World Wide Words* for a discussion of the changing meanings of the word 'meritocracy'; www.quinion.com/words/topicalwords/tw-mer1.htm. And see also Ruth Levitas's article in this issue.

people shoulder the burden and threats of social insecurity on an increasingly individualised basis, in what Ulrich Beck has described as 'the risk society'. The lottery becomes a core motif for our times.

The increasing disparity between rich and poor, the risky lottery of social opportunity, and the lack of cultural validation for many people in our society, goes a good way to explaining the expansion of interest in celebrity culture, and the eagerness with which opportunities to become a celebrity are taken up and consumed. These are some of the wider contexts in which Eminem's hymn to the fleeting moment of potential for fame is produced, in which it is bought by the truckload, and in which it clearly resonates with broader structures of feeling. *Lose Yourself* offers the image of immersion in the moment of opportunity for fame. Risk everything to lose your old self and your lack of validation; gamble your identity to acquire wealth, to become acknowledged, to become somebody.

Keeping it real: Cinderella and the celebrity work ethic

Getting to know 'the real' or 'inner' person behind or inside the celebrity has for a long time been an integral means of generating interest in them. As Richard Dyer pointed out in *Heavenly Bodies*:

> Stars are obviously a case of appearance - all we know of them is what we see and hear before us. Yet the whole media construction of stars encourages us to think in terms of 'really' - what is Crawford really like? Which biography, which word-of-mouth story, which moment in which film discloses her as she really was? The star phenomenon gathers these aspects of contemporary human existence together, laced up with the question of 'really'.[6]

The question, the enigma, of 'really' is partly what generates the cultural and economic turnover of our fascination with celebrities. It sells them, products about them and products tenuously connected to them. It informs the way we connect to celebrities, whether as abstract friends, or as offering us glimpses of what we would like to be; it offers us lifestyles we wish to inhabit, spaces of impossible longing, characteristics against which we measure ourselves, and mechanisms through which we bond with other people.

---

6. Richard Dyer, *Heavenly Bodies: Film Stars and Society*, Macmillan Press 1986, p2.

However, asking this question of what celebrities are 'really' like can matter in a range of different ways. From psychoanalytic perspectives, such a question might indicate needs or desires felt to be lacking from our own lives or psyches. From post-structuralist perspectives, it could indicate an unhealthily essentialist fetishisation symptomatic of Western logocentricism, rather than tracing multiple, interrelated developments, intensities or 'realities'. In terms of cultural history, the search to find out what celebrities are 'really' like could be understood in the context of the rise of Romanticism, possessive individualism and capitalist modernity. In these terms, the search to find out who and how celebrities 'really' are has acted as both oil to the wheels of the celebrity machine and as one of its integral motors. Similarly, the leaking of celebrity secrets has been a long-standing promotional tactic used to produce 'authentic' information which, as Dyer points out, is 'often taken to give a privileged access to the real person of the star'.[7]

Dyer's elegant and lucid analyses of film stars such as Judy Garland, Paul Robeson and Marilyn Monroe spawned a whole generation of film studies students to write essays on the construction of a particular star's image and fame. In *Stars*, Dyer influentially wrote that 'what is interesting about them is not the characters they have constructed ... but rather the business of constructing/performing/being (depending on the particular star involved) a "character"'. Reading this today, and thinking about this in a wider context from that of solely film stars, it is clear that it is not only academic and journalistic commentators who find the business of constructing celebrity fascinating. Celebrity reflexivity, or mulling over the business of being or becoming a star, has become a conspicuous preoccupation of stars themselves, as *Lose Yourself/8 Mile* indicate - along with a wide range of other cultural examples (such as *Big Brother*, or Craig David and Sting singing of the *Rise and Fall* of celebrity).

The marker of what makes a celebrity 'authentic' nowadays is often a combination of the presentation of emotional intimacy with the audience, and a degree of reflexivity about being in the position of a celebrity, with an ability to reference the legitimate 'moment before' fame. We might draw on such productions of celebrity 'normality' - such messages of how they, too, once inhabited the position of wanting to be a celebrity - not only to explore how

---

7. Richard Dyer, *Stars*, new edition, British Film Institute 1998, p61.

celebrities are 'just like us' through the way they magnify 'everyday' mannerisms or characteristics (what Couldry terms elsewhere their 'extraordinary ordinariness'), but also to think about how they are presented as being like us *in wanting to be celebrities*. For the idea that 'to be ordinary' in our culture will probably entail 'wanting to be a celebrity' in part gets reproduced and naturalised from such positions.

Clearly, referencing 'the moment before' fame is in part about money, work and class. One of the most common celebrity stories, most recently epitomised by J-Lo's *Jenny from the Block*, is the celebrity who worked his or her way up from the bottom of the social pile. The rags-to-riches tale is an age-old narrative. It is the story of Cinderella, whose basic plot elements, as Angela Carter said, 'occur everywhere from China to Northern England', wherever there is social inequality.[8] That this currency has become prominent today is not particularly surprising considering that we live in a world in which rags have become more prevalent and riches more opulent. At the same time this narrative is also inflected in some very modern ways. Thus, instead of merely luxuriating in her palatial excess, Cinderella now has to show that she can still remember that she started out in the kitchen. This knowledge or awareness structures her character; it stops her 'getting above herself', it keeps her 'real'.

The strength of such a motif in contemporary culture can be understood in relation to the neo-liberal discourse of meritocracy. Of course, just as there is plenty right in wanting people to move beyond experiences of deprivation, there is nothing wrong with not wanting to be arrogant or socially snobby (and such sentiments have become common sense now in a way they weren't even fifty years ago). But, as Stuart Hall pointed out many years ago, celebrations of 'the popular' can take many different political forms.[9] And this recognition of the place from which a celebrity has risen by no means signifies a populism which, in its appreciation of 'working-class' people and forms, wants to hold up and celebrate their image in order to make available more opportunities and resources. J-Lo's persona in *Jenny from the Block*, for example, is not constructed around what she gives back: it's what she has extracted from

---

8. Angela Carter 'Introduction' to Angela Carter (ed) *The Virago Book of Fairy Tales*, Virago 1990.
9. Stuart Hall, 'Notes on Deconstructing the Popular', in Raphael Samuel (ed) *People's History and Socialist Theory*, Routledge and Kegan Paul 1981.

the street - her 'realness', her supposed urban 'groundedness' - and has *taken away with her* that's important. It is a structure of feeling that uses its 'appreciation' for the block for entirely individualistic purposes, in order to justify enormous wealth and divest itself of any guilt, rather than to enter into a reciprocal relationship. As such it sustains, furthers and deepens inequality rather than tackles it, and is entirely congruent with what has been called 'corporate populism'.[10] What more perfect image could there be for a company to use for selling, what more potent dream could you buy into, than glamour which pretends to be democratic through-and-through?

In J-Lo's case there are of course other important explanatory factors we can draw on, in terms of gender and 'race' - reasons why it is unsurprising that a Latina singer from the Bronx might be attracted to *bling*. It has long been recognised that cultures of ostentatious wealth are ways for disenfranchised people to stick two fingers up to those who held them down and back. This is clearly visible in the thick heavy gold chains of black rappers, also worn by young white working-class boys who share their material and cultural disempowerment (and who often want to borrow what is perceived of as being their hyper-masculinity). It is also apparent in the kind of feminist discourse that, since the shoulder-padded working girls of the 1980s at least, has trumpeted ostentatious wealth as a signifier of female liberation. J-Lo offers a celebration of a materialist young feminism similar to that of the Destiny's Child anthem *Independent Women*, which celebrates 'all the honeys/that make the money'.

But to acknowledge these moves as resistant is not to accept that they are wholly progressive and emancipatory. As Don Slater has pointed out, there is a fine but deeply significant line between acknowledging that a consumer or a culture is 'active', and assuming that it is 'oppositional'. (To trace the story of the confusion over this distinction is to trace one of the stories of cultural studies.) The success of figures such as J-Lo offers one type of liberation only by annexing or connecting it to a celebratory endorsement of the profit motive of consumer capitalism. Whereas some used to think that black struggles and

---

10. For a discussion of Anthony Barnett's use of this term and related themes see Michael Rustin, 'The New Labour ethic and the spirit of capitalism' in *Soundings*, Issue 14, Spring 2000, p116.
11. Don Slater, *Consumer Culture and Modernity*, Polity Press 1997, p171.

gender struggles were, by themselves, opposed to capitalism (and they often were, since the people on the top of the pile were then wholly, instead of mainly, white, male and upper class), today it is clear that they are not. As Sheila Rowbotham, a long-term campaigner for women's liberation, poignantly puts it: 'our hopes have been appropriated, our aspirations twisted'. Identity politics became articulated to the corporate search for profit as well as the search for co-operation:

> Ironically, openings created by social movements were to present market opportunities - the slogans transmogrified into designer labels and some quick-footed 'alternative' capitalists emerged from the melee. Yet the radical dream of the sixties was to be stillborn, for we were not to move towards the co-operative egalitarian society we had imagined. Instead the sixties ushered in an order which was more competitive and less equal than the one we had protested against.[12]

Paul Gilroy talks of a similar process as 'filleting', a process by which corporate interests gut a progressive discourse 'for what they want and adapt it to the rhythms of their own complicity with consumerism'.[13]

This highlights the importance of linkages, or articulation: of the ways in which discourses can be linked, re-appropriated or co-opted for different ends, and the ways in which discourses build their power through alliances. If we are looking for what Williams called 'resources of hope', or meanings that have the potential to be re-articulated to more progressive ends, one such resource might be the widespread ridiculing of J-Lo's sentiments of being able to 'keep it real' despite her wealth. She clearly is not the same now as she was when she was much poorer, and, to many, her inability to recognise this, or to offer any affective sense of the *difficulty* of moving out of such social circumstances, is insulting to those who do live in conditions of material poverty - and to the intelligence of her audience.

Another resource might be the different types of relationship that are

---

12. Sheila Rowbotham *Promise of a Dream: Remembering the Sixties*, Penguin 2000, ppxiv-xv.
13. Marquand Smith, 'On the State of Cultural Studies: An interview with Paul Gilroy', *Third Text* 49, Winter 1999-2000, p21.

articulated between celebrities and their materially poorer 'roots'. Ms Dynamite, for instance, is often figured as exposing or highlighting awareness of the broader social issues that surround and have created racism and economic deprivation. Within the constraints of celebrity's always - by definition - individualistic nature, the Ms Dynamite example does at least offer less individualistic messages. However, this also raises important questions about whether and how celebrity can ever be used to further equalities, and, if it can't, what the alternatives to celebrity might be. As the Ms Dynamite example shows, there are many ways in which celebrities are used to promote discourses that benefit the many rather than the few. The pronouncements celebrities make, the attitudes they embody, and the identifications they make possible can all be used to instigate cultural change that engenders equality rather than exploitation. For example, from the suffragettes to the Spice Girls and beyond, many different types of feminisms have been promoted through celebrities. And non-governmental organisations are perennially keen to garner celebrity support, as this raises the news profile of an issue and engenders affective identifications.

The most obvious contemporary model of 'democratic' celebrity is probably the celebrity of the 'leader' of the Zapatistas in Mexico, Subcommandante Marcos. Masked and anonymous, this is a celebrity who everyone and anyone can claim to be, as no-one knows who he 'really' is. It is a self-consciously dissolved model of celebrity in which Marcos is everyone, sharing the fame in the same way as that other famous example when celebrity was dissolved into the populace, *Spartacus*. Stanley Kubrick's well-known 1960 epic (penned by a blacklisted screenwriter) featured other slaves taking the identity of the condemned revolutionary Roman slave-turned-hero in solidarity, so that one and all became a shared identity ('I am Spartacus!'). Analogously, the recent finale of *Buffy the Vampire Slayer* dissolved Buffy's celebrity and power into all and any potential slayers.

Yet of course, in another way, these are not so much 'alternative' models of celebrity, more its antithesis, in which the celebrity is also eradicated by being dissolved into the collectivity. Similarly, however progressive it is, Ms Dynamite's story is still represented as an *individualised* achievement. Whilst there are aspects of some celebrities that can be used or articulated in less unequal ways, structurally, 'celebrity' is always by definition individualistic: it is both a magnified example of the individualisation of our society and a key mechanism through which this process of individualisation functions. In 'Letter to a Harsh Critic' Gilles Deleuze terms 'the opposite of celebrity' as a set of liberated singularities, opening a 'self' up to the multiplicities within:

> It's a strange business, speaking for yourself, in your own name, because it doesn't at all come with seeing yourself as an ego or a person or a subject. Individuals find a real name for themselves, rather, only through the harshest exercise in depersonalization, by opening themselves up to the multiplicities everywhere within them, to the intensities running through them. A name as the direct awareness of such intensive multiplicity is the opposite of the depersonalization effected by the history of philosophy: it's depersonalization through love rather than subjection. What one says comes from the depths of one's ignorance, the depths of one's own underdevelopment. One becomes a set of liberated singularities, words, names, fingernails, things, animals, little events: quite the reverse of a celebrity.[14]

In these Deleuzian terms, as in Zapatismo, to be the opposite of a celebrity is to not seek individual fame, to not emphasise individuality, but to dissolve such individualism and open ourselves up to the multiplicities that constitute us. To return to Eminem's phrase with which I began, it is a way to 'lose yourself', though with a different inflection: not losing yourself to find a more 'authentic' individual self to market, to gain dominating power through, but to open it up to what is shared, to create mutual ownerships.

Lost and found

In our contemporary meritocratic culture, new possibilities of social and cultural transition are being produced alongside sharp inequalities of wealth and status. This is both reflected in and produced by the current predominant discourse of celebrity culture that surrounds us. In such a context, intimacy, reflexivity and dramatising the 'grounded' moment of pre-fame are key tropes through which the excitement around current celebrity culture is reproduced and maintained. All three are currently in widespread circulation, and all three are ways of making

---

14. Gilles Deleuze, 'Letter to a Harsh Critic' in *Negotiations 1972-1990*, Columbia University Press 1995, pp6-7.

fame seem ordinary, when of course, unless we are all receiving the same material and symbolic recognition, it is no such thing. At the same time, there is a multiplicity of uses to which celebrity, like anti-celebrity, can be put, and we can consider how celebrity is being used in the service of power in particular instances: whether it is being used to help shore it up or dish it out. Simultaneously, we inhabit a variety of roles as producers, consumers, creators, distributors and communicators, roles through which we combine with others to endorse, reject, remould or create what celebrity means in relation to our 'ordinary' lives.

This is a shorter version of a longer paper that appears in the new journal Mediactive, Issue 2: Celebrity. *Thanks to Jonathan Rutherford, Clare Birchall and Lynda Dyson. All websites accessed August 2003.*

Four poems

Two ways of getting lost

One. Go to Venice. Pick a stranger,
follow him through a square, down calle, cross
bridges till he turns knowingly sharp right
somewhere too dark for you to follow.
Find it's an hour's walk from your hotel, an hour
till the door locks against you for the night. Find it's too dark
under the streetlights to read the map,
that all these alleys end in water.

Two. This is harder. Stay home. Become a stranger
in your own town. Find routine makes you trivial and cross,
your paper no longer seems a bastion, or right.
Find the grass grows wild and the clematis won't follow
the wires you set for it, that each hour
shrinks according to the task; that even the familiar dark
brings little comfort. Finally, set out without provisions or a map,
find a river that you've never known was there, listen for the
wind on water.

Elizabeth Foy

The Chapel of the Virgin Mary

There. In forever twilight.
   The faint caesium glow

of her cape. Face white
   as lead. Those decades

strung along her rosary's
   suspension of atoms - how

they snag the small light!
   Miraculous - one tear

starts down her cheek -
   Heavy Water. That

bent finger she points
   to a porcelain heart.

And always her eyes -
   the way they tilt to where

an infant might rest - that
   bloodless cradle which is

her hollow of breast.
   The old ones say - *See her*

and die. All who kneel
   there know - she too

once held a child
   that would not cry.

Mario Petrucci

Meeting up at Fingal's bridge

Just as our own, the river's origins seemed lost
on some winter-land of edge-less moor
though we shared one source, a same forgotten past
picking our way from one fragile mooring
of small talk to another as the dippers
perched on makeshift islands and the river
whispering, lisping alongside, linked
the moments as they lapsed or fell apart;

but suddenly, instantly together, we saw the tree
flame orange against the darkening steep
glowing with the rising sap as if it breathed
the voice of a prophet; then suddenly, closer up,
astonishing us, the halo vanished, leaving
the tree as the rest - a winter mesh of iron;
then backing off we saw it flame again, a trick
we saw in unison, siblings, at last met up

as we'd jointly heard the river's lisped
soliloquies linking our own unspoken ones.
So we all got together, loud, convivial
in the easy timelessness of the beauty spot;
feeling now behind the words the pull
of water, winter light, the halo from the rising sap
the trick of its vanishing; the river lisping on
into the darkness and the dippers folded
away some place for the night to come.

Judy Gahagan

Nuns

After I watched an Italian film
about a broken hearted woman
who became a nun I had a sense
for just a few minutes, walking
over Hungerford Bridge from
the National Film Theatre,
of what it might be like not to care
if anybody ever loved me again
because I had chosen to love Jesus
and I think what I felt was peace

so on the night I had to dress for
a Murder Mystery Dinner
as a glamorous nun I wondered
if I might get that feeling again,
but I was a moll disguised as a Sister
and all I felt was upset after my friend,
whose husband was my gangster lover,
told me I looked good in a habit
and I knew I was doomed with my
novice's body, floozy's heart.

Lorraine Mariner

The last of the great French Marxists?

John Cowley

Henri Lefebvre, *Critique of Everyday Life: Foundations for a Sociology of the Everyday Volume II*, Verso 2002

This volume of *Critique of Everyday Life* was first published in Paris in 1961, not long after the 1956 revelations by Khrushchev to the Twentieth Congress of the Communist Party of the Soviet Union and Russia's intervention into Hungary that same year. These had been seismic events for left intellectuals, with many of them turning against not only the Communist Party but also Marxism. Not so Lefebvre. Although excluded from the Party in 1958, having been long berated for his 'neo-Hegelianism', theoretical inconsistencies and general waywardness in his thinking, he continued to search for a critical active engagement with the world. He deplored the dogmatism of the Communist Parties as intellectual death. But he retained the expectation of the possible renewal of the struggle for socialism within the Soviet bloc countries. Like Karl Korsch and Antonio Gramsci before him, Lefebvre wished to hold on to the vital threads, the critical intent, of dialectical thinking. The 'revolutionary principle is essentially critical (negative) … today it applies more to everyday life than to knowledge in general or to society in general; this is our way of reintroducing science into praxis' (p186). He was writing at the very start of the 1960s; later events, especially those of May 1968, were confirmation that he was pursuing the right course.

The book seeks to set the course for a rigorous and critical approach to post-war society. The search is for a deeper understanding of the everyday, of how the life of the individual forever engages itself in the life of the society. The project is both extremely complex and intellectually demanding. What makes this particular volume so extraordinary is that it entails a wide-ranging interrogation of the moment of crisis as it unfolds in the 1960s, giving insight into the events that are to come in 1968, the 'ideas of May'. Lefebvre explores the theoretical categories necessary for understanding the emerging world of consumerism then enveloping the individual, involving the strangest of emotional entrapments, as well as the possibilities of resistance. It is precisely this prescience which makes the text so remarkable and worthy of republishing. In his quest to locate, open to understanding, the reality of what is happening, Lefebvre critically examines structuralism, existentialism, linguistics, semiotics, even the possibilities of a textual reading of urban daily life, forever reminding the reader of the dangers inherent in any retreat from a direct critical *engagement* with the world in all its complexity and contradictions. He recognises the enticements of merely seeking to interpret culture, highlighting the dangers of pursuing insights one-sidedly, leaving behind theoretical rigour for descriptive commentaries. This argument is an extraordinary anticipation of the actual post-1960s retreat into cultural studies - which offers a critique without engagement - and of post-modernism's interpretations without history or possibilities.

Although written over forty years ago, so much of what Lefebvre questions is topical. He recognises the fundamental significance of 'Otherness' to human perception, the importance of 'globalization' and what he calls 'globalized society', as well as the 'total alienation of the everyday', all the time seeking to unravel the significance of the everyday for societal and individual life. He points to the centrality of the urban street in revealing the internal and external aspects of alienation in contemporary life. Women, he writes, 'in general bear the weight of everyday life' (p115). He reflects on the withdrawal into a more private everyday, of the family and dwelling, with its burden of housework, and what this means for women: 'They are its everyday critique' (p223).

Lefebvre wanted to push sociology beyond descriptive monologues on class and gender inequalities and the social problems of post-war capitalist societies.

What was needed was a critical engagement with the way in which consumer society exploits, penetrates, manipulates, and envelops the individual in everyday life, the monotony and emptiness, reaching deep inside the 'social individual'. The life of the individual expresses itself in the 'rhythms' and 'nucleuses', repetitions and routines, 'which make up the immediacy of everyday'. Rather than direct repression, it is a matter of everyday sociality, the place of social reproduction, of consuming, the illusions of pleasure and choice. It involves an internalised disciplining, of routines and habituation, so the present presses down, a monotony, drudgery, and self-repression. Even the attempt to find oneself against all of that involves alienation. The living contradiction of the everyday is that it is 'non-essential', yet it is all that 'matters to mankind' (p336).

Lefebvre's searching for the possibilities of engagement, critique, desires and hopes, dreams and imaginings, brings to mind the title of Milan Kundera's novel *The Unbearable Lightness of Being*. The imposed disciplines of the lived everyday excuse us, allowing participation in our own repression. Henri Lefebvre was involved in a life-long search for socialism, seeking to uncover the frustrated needs, hidden desires, hopes and dreams contained within the everyday lives of people, buried deep within their social life, yet clearly there: seeking movement towards the transformation of everyday life with all the many possibilities it contains. These suppressed hopes originate in the lived experiences of ordinary life. In France these hopes have historically found expression in the play and artistic exuberance of the Festival, long dreamed of by many, and on occasions demonstrated, as in 1790 during the French Revolution, and again in the Paris Commune of 1871 - seventy-three extraordinary days in spring, when the people took to the streets of Paris, creating a Festival of dazzling simplicity (and then again in May 1968). These are the moments in which are briefly glimpsed the myriad possibilities of people freely associating together. Festival is a re-occurring theme in Lefebvre's writings.

Henrie Lefebvre died in 1991, having been a highly creative and active force in French political and intellectual life for most of the twentieth century. He wrote more than sixty books, always engaging with the intellectual challenges of the day and confronting the stances of the more iconic figures of France such as Jean-Paul Sartre, Guy Debord, Michel Foucault and Louis Althusser. Lefebvre's influence is worldwide, yet many academics are unaware of their debt. This last of the French Marxists, as he once called himself, has at least escaped being embalmed by academia.

Stories about stories

Debra Benita Shaw

Donna Haraway, *The Companion Species Manifesto: Dogs, People, and Significant Otherness*, Prickly Paradigm Press 2003
Sarah Kember, *Cyberfeminism and Artificial Life*, Routledge 2003
Jane Miller, *Relations*, Jonathan Cape 2003

For Donna Haraway, 'understanding the world is about living inside stories' (*How Like A Leaf*, 2000). But no story about the world can be universally and ahistorically true. Haraway's stories refer us to habituation; to the sense in which we both inhabit and routinely internalise and rehearse the narratives of origin which structure what counts as knowledge in the developed West. When, in 1985, she wrote 'the cyborg is our ontology', she invited those of us who had always been other to the coherent, masculine, white subject of these origin stories to write ourselves into the lived reality of the late twentieth century. The cyborg celebrated the pollution of naturalised categories in a post-cold war world populated with technoscientific and biotechnological entities like genes, bytes and retroviruses. Central to Haraway's argument is the challenge to the biopolitics of Darwinian taxonomy provided by the epistemological paradigm emerging from the ascendancy of information technologies. The cyborg is not only intimate with machines but must acknowledge kinship with other forms of life with whom we share the code, the genome, the description of 'life' as we currently understand it; animals, bacteria and, more recently, Artificial Life or what Sarah Kember refers to as 'Alife' (pvii), 'embodied computer programs, situated autonomous robots and transgenic organisms' (pviii).

In *Cyberfeminism and Artificial Life*, feminism, whether cyber or otherwise, is often assumed rather than spelled out in the analysis. Nevertheless, Kember clearly maintains a cyborg position throughout her critique, articulated through a carefully formulated overview of the biopolitics of Alife research and its consumer products. Cyborg politics have too often been assumed to be a natural corollary of posthumanism, leading to, for instance, Carol A Stabile's charge that 'the cyborg feminist need not *do* anything in order to be political' (*Feminism and the Technological Fix*). What Kember demonstrates is that this is emphatically not the case. Indebted to Richard Dawkins's *The Selfish Gene*, 'ALife allegorises creation and the fall and is attuned to the narratives of *Frankenstein* and *Faust* through which it connects with molecular biology, especially genomics' (p81). Alife is 'emergent' in the sense that, unlike Artificial Intelligence, which depends on complex programmes which attempt to mimic human thought processes, it 'evolves spontaneously and from the bottom up through interaction with the artificial environment' (p3). But most programmes, from Dawkins's own Biomorph to computer games like *SimLife* and *SimEarth*, offer a Darwinian model of evolution and development, in which competition for available resources and a basic heterosexual model of reproduction are fundamental. The posthuman, in these scenarios, is simply that which, despite blurring the boundaries between nature and culture, human and machine, and organic and prosthetic, nevertheless reproduces deterministic discourses in which gender and sexuality are simply assumed. Kember's critique is, in itself, an example of what the cyborg feminist needs to do, but she finds other examples, for instance in Jane Prophet, Gordon Selley and Mark Hurry's *TechnoSphere*, an artificial ecosystem on the Internet, inhabited by creatures with 'only one sex and [...] no gender' (p131).

For Kember, the concept of autopoiesis ('from Greek, meaning self-producing') offers a promising epistemological stance from which to counter the sociobiology of Alife and genomics. 'One of the central questions raised through autopoiesis', according to Kember, 'is that of the relationship between autopoietic entities and their environment ... this relationship is both autonomous and coupled, dependent but discrete' (p200). Autopoietic entities are only such because of the environment in which they exist, but they are neither determined nor formed by it, but produce themselves out of the materials that it provides. They thus offer a rather wonderful analogy for the kind of political work that the cyborg was designed to do.

For Haraway, the cyborg was an appropriate myth/metaphor in 'Reagan's

Star Wars times of the mid-1980s' (p4). Now, at the turn of the millennium, she has other stories to tell. *The Companion Species Manifesto* goes 'to the dogs, literally' (p5) to narrate tales which retrieve the history of canine/human companionship in the service of 'science studies and feminist theory in the present time' (p5). As a reply, perhaps, to those critics for whom the cyborg was too readily associated with technophilia and the displacement of the human by the machine, Haraway offers her own dogs as living reminders of the embeddedness of companion animals in the evolution of culture. Ms Cayenne Pepper and Roland Dog appear in the text as exuberant examples of species relating and the complexity of behaviours, affects and kinships which it entails.

In *Primate Visions* Haraway wrote a feminist history of primatology, introduced by a critique of 'teddy bear patriarchy', which insists that our genetic kinship with apes is reflected in ape culture, and that ape sexuality and gender hierarchies (as perceived) serve to naturalise the power relationships of the patriarchal family. But ape geographies and ecologies are perhaps too hyperrealised and distanced in contemporary Western culture to function heuristically in mapping the complexities of what Haraway calls 'naturecultures' (p12). Dogs live, work and play *with* us. More so than cats, they are deeply imbricated in the historical structuring of culture through their roles in farming, warfare, medicine and the space race. They are pets, companions, guides and teachers and function to instruct us that 'domestication' is a loaded concept, 'the paradigmatic act of masculine, single-parent, self-birthing, whereby man makes himself repetitively as he invents (creates) his tools' (p27). Like the ape 'families' which populate the annals of popular science, dogs have been appropriated to stand for the ascendancy of culture over nature; but dog demographies tell other stories.

Haraway's 'favourite trope' for her 'dog tales' is 'metaplasm', a word 'from the Greek *metaplasmos*, meaning remodelling or remolding', and used to mean 'a change in a word, for example by adding, omitting, inverting, or transposing its letters, syllables or sounds' (p20). Haraway enjoys the 'biological taste' (p20) of the word, which she appropriates to mean 'the remodelling of dog and human flesh, remolding the codes of life, in the history of companion-species relating' (p20). Metaplasms abound in the dog world, for instance in the stories of Great Pyrenees and Australian

Shepherds, breeds emerging from complex histories which make nonsense of the concept of linear genetic inheritance or, indeed, of nature as a raw resource for culture. These are stories of opportunism, the merging of dog and human cultures as both adapt to cohabitation, and the changing meanings of breed designations as they are re-defined in terms of changes in political economy. Kennel club standards, for instance, often refer more to the values of a consumer economy than to the optimum requirements for a breed in its past as a herder or livestock guardian. Dogs, it seems, are not tamed wolves but an evolutionary divergence responsive to both human needs and their own. Haraway writes of 'co-evolution' and 'co-constitutive companion species' (p32), attentive to the metaplasmic effects of historical change, the diversification of both human and dog populations and their consequent effects on what counts in the game of survival, for both species.

Attentive, also, to the facts of her stories, rather than the abstractions which often serve to naturalise evolutionary tales, Haraway pays homage to her sports writer father, whose job was to 'tell what happened by spinning a story that is just the facts' (p18). Hence the interspersed 'Notes of A Sports Writer's Daughter' that tell anecdotes of her life with Cayenne and Roland. But these do not serve only to illustrate exactly what Haraway means when she writes about the way that dog and human lives are co-constitutive. At the heart of her manifesto is a critique of the gene fetishism she first described in *Modest_Witness@Second_Millennium.FemaleMan©_Meets_OncoMouse*™, in which the gene as symbolic phallus stands for 'life itself'. In the same way that Kember utilises the concept of autopoiesis, so Haraway inherits from her father a technique which might tell of other ways that life can be constituted. She and Cayenne 'make each other up in the flesh' (p3), in the lived reality of the physical and social negotiations which the significant otherness of species relating entails. This, then, is the cyborg writing that Haraway called for in her first manifesto; writing that disrupts the codes of style and genre, enabling the telling of stories which challenge what it means to be 'made up in the flesh'.

In this, there are significant correspondences with Jane Miller's *Relations*, the story of a family for whom writing, it could be argued, was 'life itself'. Miller speculates that her great-aunt, the celebrated Miss Collett, the first woman fellow of University College, may have been prompted to compile her extensive family archive because she was 'as puzzled by the idea of families as

I have sometimes been' (p200). *Relations* seems to be an attempt to think through this puzzlement. As she says, 'it was perverse of my parents to marry each other' (p226). Her father, although not 'completely, only, homosexual' (p20), had 'homosexual sympathies', and her mother admitted to being 'a bit homosexual too' (p21). It may, of course, be the case that Miller's parents' marriage was no less perverse than many others. Like Haraway, she tells the facts, which speak volumes about the social pressures that structure inheritance, but which are too often related in terms which confirm the mythology of Darwinian romance. Miller's mother was a painter and her father a concert pianist, and it is their identification of themselves as artists which emerges as the basis of negotiation for their relationship, both with each other and with the social milieu in which they found themselves.

M iller's mother, Ruth, was a Jew who 'married out', greatly disappointing her father, Redcliffe Salaman, a Zionist and in his time a noted scientist, who in 1949 published *The History and Social Influence of the Potato*. Miller writes that his secretary, a Miss Hagger, 'more than anyone, understood the link between Jews and potatoes, which was, as she put it, that "both involve problems of heredity"' (p36). Salaman's Zionism was founded in 'a (relatively) benign eugenics' (p45), which held that 'the best Jewish "types"' (p45), in the right environment, 'would show superior adaptability, intelligence and determination' (p45); but his pioneering work on potatoes was as concerned with the social effects of malnutrition and poverty and the deleterious effects of relying on a single source of food, as with the breeding of superior varieties. Like Haraway, then, Salaman was concerned with 'naturecultures'; with the way in which the genetic history of the potato was inseparable from 'particular forms and manifestations of poverty, and on the social arrangements that had produced them' (p38).

Interestingly, Salaman's bequest to his daughter Ruth seems to have been abstracted from his belief in the extraordinary potential of the Jews. Miller writes, almost as an aside, that she had been a disappointment to her mother, as had her sisters, whom she regarded as 'ordinary people', 'non-artists, fitters-in, good at unimportant things like driving cars, using computers and tidying up' (p16). That Ruth failed to recognise the extraordinary potential of writing is illustrated by her rather callous lack of concern when, presented with a typescript copy of one of Miller's books, she allowed the pages to fall and scatter 'irretrievably beneath [her] bed' (p23). Nevertheless, it is her daughter's art which brings this somewhat disparate family into fascinating perspective. At one point she writes that her father 'enjoyed the thought of family as one kind of window on the past', and that 'he kept the letters written to his grandfather by Karl Marx in his sock drawer, his own Fort Knox' (p228). What both sides of Miller's family seem to have shared is this sense of family as a repository of certain kinds of knowledge about the world. *Relations* tells many stories, not only about kinship and inheritance but about the relationships between science and art, social class and religion, colonialism and the perversity of English national identity. These then, are, like Haraway's dog tales, 'stories about stories, all the way down. Woof' (Haraway, p21).

Images of war

Sylvie Prasad

Jenny Matthews, *Women and War*, Pluto Press, 2003

To record global conflict from a woman's perspective, although not entirely unique, is still something of a rarity in photography. Jenny Matthews studied at the University of Sussex, worked for the British council in Brazil, and, after a spell teaching in a London comprehensive, became a successful photographer. *Women and War* represents a project extending over twenty years, from a first commission from Christian Aid to 'document the lives of women'. First presented as a collection in a major exhibition, the body of work has now been brought together in this book. Matthews presents world conflict not as a complete record of events, but as her own personal take on recent history - 'recognising the lives of remarkable women, ordinary people surviving as best as they can' (p7).

Images of war can be challenging to the viewer, particularly when detached from the immediacy of reportage and recycled on gallery walls or in 'coffee-table' monographs. As such, Martha Rossler, in her 1981 article 'In, around, and afterthoughts (on documentary photography)' was right to think the 'aesthetic-historical' moment would dominate. Without the specificity of the historical context of their construction and reception, meanings get 'fixed' by their aesthetic value. This is not to say that they lose their power to shock, disturb or even disgust; but this makes it easier, as Rossler suggests, to handle a disturbing subject by 'leaving it behind'.

Jenny Matthews works within a particular documentary tradition, which aims, as she says, to 'poke away at the world and record the way some things are, but shouldn't be' (p5). Its roots lie in the specific historical climate of early twentieth century liberal sensibilities. Documentary was and still is as much about the photographer as it is about images. Debates about realism aside, it is the intentions behind the creation of images that become points of contestation. Increasingly, socially minded intentions get displaced in a commodified culture of the 'named' artist. But, unlike many monographs depicting images of war, *Women and War* is no ego trip for the photographer. A considered balance exists between testimony - the voices of those who might otherwise go unheard - and authored images and commentary.

From the outset, Matthews's role as photographer is also made clear. She makes no claims for objective reality; indeed, the back cover of the book reinforces her particular part in the triangle between 'viewer' and 'viewed'. The cover depicts two images of a woman with her baby taken in Mozambique. The first image verges on the cliché, with the camera looking down on its passive subject. The second image is more uplifting, though no less tragic in its circumstances. Matthews explains: 'She looked the part of the war-weary refugee, dressed only in a sack, her baby desperately trying to feed, but as soon as she became aware of the camera, her demeanour changed completely - she became the beatific mother. Both images happened, both images are true'.

It is this honesty in foregrounding the very real but mutually manipulative relationship between photographer and subject that gives this book its critical edge. Matthews highlights the complexities and the politics involved in representation, without presenting an overly academic analysis. Seducing the reader into acknowledging that there is more than one 'truth' can make us aware of other conventions that are silently operating to make this a 'serious' text. Black and white images, and the absence of colour reproductions (Matthews does her own darkroom work), are further confirmation of the 'validity' of the document and the primacy of the photographer's project to depict what is there. However, for me, it is not just the conventions she works within that give credibility to the images, it is, rather, the return to questions of ethics. Jenny Matthews engages with her subjects - a dialogue with a clear sense of responsibility, in which others are allowed to speak. Without such intentions there is always a danger of a photograph exploiting those not in a position to protest. There are, in this book, the stereotypical 'victim' pictures we are only too familiar with in war imagery, but these are few in number. Between the diary entries, the photographs and the personal testimonies of the women themselves, Matthews weaves together a complex narrative of women and conflict.

While women are often the victims of war, they are increasingly taking another part on the front line and becoming killers. This paradox, of women as bearers of life, as mothers, sits uneasily with their roles as tank drivers or guerrillas. Marta, a 14-year-old from Nicaragua, is pictured looking contemplative in army uniform, Kalashnikov slung over her left shoulder. The accompanying diary entry tells us she has been in the reserves for a year (p117). Two male soldiers dressed identically flank twenty-year-old Rocio, a Spanish soldier serving with the UN. Her role as an equal beside the men working on traffic convoys is made explicit. Part diary, part commentary, part testimony *Women and War* builds up to much more than a photographic record of events. Many of the images become 'life affirming', often by their ordinariness, and in spite of the violence which surrounds them. Croatia 3 December 1991, diary entry: 'Marisa beating the hell out of her washing in the freezing mist, mortars booming in the background' (p100). The accompanying image is strikingly beautiful. Mist rises above shimmering waters, with December trees silhouetted against the sky - the figure of a woman headscarfed, aproned, back to the camera, wringing out her washing. The aesthetics are there but the text firmly anchors the image to its context.

El Salvador: two white-haired women, heads bent, engrossed with pencils and paper, learning to read and write for the first time. The pleasure of witnessing this moment, captured through the lens, is fixed by the words on the page. The diary entry reads: ' I am totally overwhelmed' (p56). There are numerous images such as these - a woman feeding pigeons, women fixing their make-up, crying, laughing, providing points of identification for all of us, juxtaposed between things we might only half imagine.

Not altogether successful in portraying the magnitude of the events it seeks to represent is a mound of guns on one page, mirrored on the adjacent page by a pile of bones - victims of the Rwandan conflict (pp42-43). The physical space reduced to a two-dimensional form becomes an exercise in page layout to gain maximum emotional impact. A more successful juxtaposition is in the photographs from Gaza 2002 (pp108-109). One image shows a young boy dying from gunshot wounds at a checkpoint; the facing page is a beauty salon, with Nadia in her wedding dress getting her hair done. The placing of these images, while deliberate, does not simply shock, but emphasises that even in times of uncertainty life goes on - a continuing theme throughout the book. It is in the depicting of these tiny rituals of the everyday that the subtext becomes a celebration of human determination and spirit.

Lest we think these images are all too remote and from far away places, I was brought up short by a photograph of Clissold Park, North London, two minutes from my own front door. November 1997 - Mimi, an Algerian journalist, plays with her children, waiting to hear if she has been granted asylum.

One of the criticisms of war photography is that people get fixed in time and place. We never get to know the subsequent fate of the people in the images, what happens to those who survive conflicts only to become frozen in the public eye, icons of a particular moment in history. Matthews occasionally fills in those details. Angela, the illegal immigrant, is the cleaner of the family Matthews stays with in the USA (p57). The irony of this situation is not lost on the author or the reader. Conflicts all too often mean displaced people. Some of those may eventually become our neighbours or our hired domestic help.

Documentary as 'revolutionary politics' will probably not be found between the pages of this book, but neither are we put in the easy position of simply 'leaving it behind'.

Merry-go-round of death

Cynthia Cockburn

Every two years, the UK plays host to an international 'arms trade fair', the Defence Systems Equipment International (DSEi). In September 2003, arms buyers from all over the world were invited to London's Excel Centre to shop for guns and tanks, military aircraft and artillery, mines and small arms. The government spent £420 million of taxpayers' money in twelve months on supporting the sale of arms, and subsidised DSEi by £1.5 million.

In the photos here and on the front cover, Women in Black against War portray this so-called 'fair' as a sinister merry-go-round. 'Roll up, roll up! Buy your candy floss and take your pick of all the most up to date methods of killing and controlling people'. WIB's leaflet protested that - putting British companies' profitability above morality and responsibility - the government permits arms sales to regimes with appalling human rights records, countries that are at war with each other, and to the world's poorest regions, where public spending should be on education, health, food and housing. The street drama focused attention particularly on small arms, 10 per cent of the 'legal' global arms trade. Handguns sell like hot cakes at the DSEi fair and are often implicated in violence against women.

Women in Black called on the UK government to stop licensing arms exports, convert the weapons industry to socially-responsible production, support multilateral disarmament and ban the sale of hand guns.

Women in Black against War is an international network. Further information from <wibinfo@gn.apc.org> and <www.womeninblack.org.uk>.

Photography: Cynthia Cockburn

From a 9-panel exhibition 'Lying, Sitting, Standing, Stepping: Some Women's Actions for Peace and Justice 1995-2003', *available for loan. Enquiries* <*wibinfo@gn.apc.org*>.

As we lay on the cobbles of Covent Garden, it began to rain.

For Edward Said

Stuart Hall

*This appreciation of Edward Said, the distinguished
literary scholar, cultural critic and courageous
advocate for the cause of the Palestinian people,
was first given at the opening of the Oxford staging
of the IniVA exhibition The Veil.[1] The exhibition was
dedicated to Said, who died in November 2003 at
the age of 67, after a twelve year struggle with
leukaemia.*

Edward Said was born in Jerusalem in 1935. His father was a Palestinian
Christian who emigrated to the US in 1911, became an American citizen
and fought with the US army in France in the First World War. The family
moved to Cairo, where Wadie Said established a successful business, and
Edward - who was named after the Prince of Wales - was sent to Victoria
College, an English language public-school-style institution, the 'Eton of
the Middle East'. He had a classic middle-class colonial childhood. His father
was stern, over-bearing and distant. His mother, the daughter of a Baptist
missionary from Nazareth, adored Edward - and the feeling was mutual.
Nevertheless, she was a somewhat manipulative, and emotionally baffling,
figure, who left him feeling that her expectations of him always went
unfulfilled. Though manifestly clever, he found it hard to fit in, was rarely

---

1. *The Veil*, an exhibition mounted by InIVA (The Institute of International Visual Arts),
   featured contemporary artists who deploy the motif of 'veiling' and 'the veil' in their
   work. It opened at the Walsall Gallery and showed at Modern Art Oxford, before going
   on tour. The catalogue publication, *Veil: Veiling, Representation and Contemporary Art*, is
   available from institute@iniva.org.

praised, and was often identified as a troublesome boy, requiring discipline; he quickly came to experience himself - as he later put it in the title of his moving memoir of his childhood - permanently *'Out Of Place'*. He said later that the tensions in his family induced a split between his outer self, and the 'loose, irresponsible, fantasy-ridden metamorphoses of my private inner life'. The family was comfortably off, however, and lived and travelled in style. Edward was sent to the US to Mount Hermon School in Massachusetts, where the earlier pattern was repeated - blossoming academically, but - again - never quite fitting in. He was trained at the Princeton and Harvard graduate schools in the European tradition of Comparative Literature and began teaching at Columbia in 1963, an institution which he never left.

The Six Days War of 1967 was the watershed experience of his life, transforming the scholar and critic into a person with deep, abiding and unshakeable political convictions. Thereafter, he became publicly identified with the cause of the Palestinian people. Increasingly controversial, and libellously attacked, he fought a relentless struggle - in books like *The Question of Palestine* and *Covering Islam*, and in a stream of articles and essays - against the way the plight of the Palestinians was misrepresented, especially in the American media and by the right-wing pro-Israel lobby in the US. His book, *After The Last Sky*, with the photographs of Jean Moir, eloquently evoked the refugee life of ordinary Palestinians expelled from their homeland.

Edward served as an independent member of the Palestinian National Council, was an early supporter of the two-state solution, and always - and consistently - was committed to the larger hope of a possible future in which Palestinian and Jew could live peacefully together. He devoted much of his life and writing to this wider purpose, which however never led him to qualify his advocacy of the rightfulness of the Palestinians' basic claims to rights of settlement in a home of their own. He helped draft President Arafat's address to the General Assembly of the UN in 1984. He came to regard the Oslo Agreements as little short of 'a Palestinian Versailles'. However, he became openly and progressively critical of the Arafat leadership, of its authoritarian features and its widespread corruption, regarding it as having failed to offer its people a principled or democratic leadership. He was accordingly shunned in

Arafat's inner circles, where he was - ironically - advised to 'go back to literature'. Said's early work, in books like *Beginnings* and *The World, The Text and the Critic*, developed a distinctive critical methodology. He was a brilliantly gifted and incisive critic. His breadth of interest was remarkably wide, and he brought this to bear in a consistently insightful way on writers and texts. His engagement with the literary and cultural life of his times - registered in his many critical commentaries and reviews on major texts, thinkers, and ideas - was impressive, in an age in which criticism has largely lost its bearings in a wider intellectual and political world. He was committed to the secular, 'worldly' intellectual life as a vocation. Literature, culture and politics fused at an early stage of his intellectual development, and his finest work was created out of that rich matrix.

It has been argued that Said's strong sense of his own marginal and exilic status enabled him to adopt a kind of 'double-consciousness' in his readings of works in the great western literary canon. Thus his study *Joseph Conrad and the Fiction of Autobiography* was keenly alive to Conrad's complicated and ambivalent position as chronicler *and* critic of Empire. He was able to appreciate the ways in which the canon's great achievements - Jane Austen's *Mansfield Park* or Conrad's *Heart of Darkness,* Forster's *Passage to India* or Kipling's *Kim* - were *both* profoundly embedded in their own historicity and shaped by their moment and culture, *and*, at the same time, remarkable achievements of human awareness, depth of insight and complexity. He never fell into a crude and simplistic either/or, for or against: 'not masterpieces that have to be venerated, but … works that have to be grasped in their historical density so that they can resonate'.

His most influential and innovative work was undoubtedly *Orientalism*, published in 1978. This book single-handedly created, and remains amongst the foremost texts of, what is now called 'post-colonial studies'. Based on an astonishing breadth of reading in English and French, this book demonstrated how 'Orientalist' scholarship and discourse had constructed and produced 'the Orient', in the two centuries following Napoleon's conquest of Egypt, as both an object of knowledge and a site for the exercise of power. This work demonstrated how the systematic mis-representations which he had uncovered in the regular western media reporting on the Middle East were in fact 'part of a much larger system of thought that was endemic to the West's whole enterprise of dealing with the Arab world'. His working-through of this insight has proved to be one of the most illuminating and compelling modern critical insights. It is still very widely drawn on, having changed the fundamental paradigm of thought about the imperial imagination - often by critics who, while standing on the back of this hard-won perception, cannot bring themselves to name its source. In answer to the criticism that this presented too binary a picture, his second instalment of the argument - *Culture and Imperialism*, published in 1993 - bent the twig in the opposite direction, stressing, through a remarkable series of studies of major political intellectuals of the de-colonising world such as C.L.R. James and Frantz Fanon, how inseparably inter-twined were the fates and fortunes of margin and metropole, coloniser and colonised, in the history of Empire and its aftermath.

In the last years and months of his life, he wrote more, more urgently and on a wider range of topics than ever before. He brought together selections of his essays and reviews in collections like *Reflections On Exile*, and of his political journalism in *The End of The Peace Process*. He also published his wonderful lecture *Freud and the Non-Europeans*, which not only sympathetically explores Freud's complicated identification with 'Jewishness' but also - through its interrogation of Freud's text *Moses and Monotheism*, on the origins of mono-theism in Christianity, Judaism and Islam, and its exploration of the Egyptian background to Moses - symbolically opens a pathway to the possible common ground between the so intimately connected, yet so hostile and opposed, 'worlds' of Arab and Jew. In his joint work with his friend Daniel Barenboim in establishing the West-Eastern Divan orchestra, and his writings on Wagner and other composers in *Musical Elaborations*, he returned to his deep love for and involvement with music - he was an accomplished pianist of near-professional standard - deploying it as an instrument of international understanding and collaboration.

A wonderfully warm and open friend and colleague, a critic of fierce integrity and sound judgement, a figure committed to the vocation of critical public intellectual, a commanding political intellectual and a person of passionate and courageous political commitment, his loss is devastating in both public and personal terms. Our common lives have been deeply enriched and inspired by his life and work. The gap he leaves behind is immeasurable. We shall be lucky to see his like again.

A Positive Agenda For Public Services

Taking the debate forward

Catalyst Public Services Programme 2004

Building on a number of important and influential interventions in recent debates around public service reform, Catalyst is developing a programme of research activities aimed at moving that debate forward into new positive and progressive territory.

Catalyst's Public Services Programme will aim to facilitate and stimulate a productive and inclusive dialogue among:

- individuals, organisations and communities that use on and interact with public services
- staff and professionals who work in public services, and the trade unions who represent them
- progressive researchers, analysts and commentators from academia, the media and the policy community

At the heart of this discussion will be an attempt to focus on the dynamic and multidimensional relationship between those who use public services and those who deliver them. We hope to draw from this a set of shared principles, understandings and objectives that can help shape a positive agenda for public services in the years ahead.

continues overleaf

continued from previous page

Our ultimate goal is to help inform and guide the process of building a broad and sustainable political and social coalition of support for

- maintaining high and increasing levels of investment in public services funded through fair and redistributive taxation
- a renewal of those services that develops the benefits of a strong public service ethos and a culture of equal and participatory social citizenship

The first stage of this project will be a series of **policy seminars** bringing together key representatives of the groups above to review experience and refine ideas on key topics:

- Why public services?
- Public service users: experiences and perspectives
- Public service workers: experiences and perspectives
- Responsive public services: how can users best be empowered?
- Ownership and control: how can structures affect delivery?

These seminars will feed a parallel programme of in-house research, the initial outcome of which will be presented for wider debate in autumn 2004 at a major **national conference** being organised with the Barry Amiel and Norman Melburn Trust, and bringing together a large participating audience of Catalyst supporters, trades unionists, civil society organisations, grass roots activists, and engaged citizens and service users.

We intend this to be an organic and increasingly inclusive process and we will at all stages welcome feedback on the above and offers of intellectual contribution. For more information or to get involved please contact Catherine Needham by emailing **catherine.needham@catalystforum.org.uk** or call **020 7733 2111**.

BACK ISSUES

Issue 1 - Launch Issue - Stuart Hall/ Beatrix Campbell/ Fred Halliday/ Mae-Wan Ho/ Barbara Castle/ Simon Edge.

Issue 2 - Law & Justice, editor Bill Bowring - contributors - Kate Markus, Keir Starmer, Ken Wiwa, Kader Asmal, Mike Mansfield, Jonathan Cooper, Ethan Raup, John Griffith, Keith Ewing, Ruth Lister and Anna Coote. Plus Steven Rose/ Jeffrey Weeks/ David Bell.

Issue 3 - Heroes & Heroines - contributors - Barbara Taylor, Jonathan Rutherford, Graham Dawson, Becky Hall, Anna Grimshaw, Simon Edge, Kirsten Notten, Susannah Radstone, Graham Martin and Cynthia Cockburn. Plus Anthony Barnett/ David Donnison/ John Gill and Nick Hallam.

Issue 4 - The Public Good - editor Maureen Mackintosh - contributors - Gail Lewis, Francie Lund, Pam Smith, Loretta Loach, John Clarke, Jane Falkingham, Paul Johnson, Will Hutton, Charlie King, Anne Simpson, Brigid Benson, Candy Stokes, Anne Showstack Sassoon, Sarabajaya Kumar, Ann Hudock, Carlo Borzaga and John Stewart. Plus Paul Hirst, Grahame Thompson/ Anne Phillips/ Richard Levins

Issue 5 - Media Worlds - editors Bill Schwarz and David Morley - contributors - James Curran, Sarah Benton, Esther Leslie, Angela McRobbie, David Hesmondhalgh, Jonathan Burston, Kevin Robins, Tony Dowmunt and Tim O'Sullivan. Plus Phil Cohen/ Duncan Green/ Cynthia Cockburn.

Issue 6 - 'Young Britain' - editor Jonathan Rutherford - contributors - Jonathan Keane, Bilkis Malek, Elaine Pennicott, Ian Brinkley, John Healey, Frances O'Grady, Rupa Huq, Michael Kenny and Peter Gartside. Plus Miriam Glucksmann/ Costis Hadjimichalis/ Joanna Moncrieff.

Issue 7 - States of Africa - editors Victoria Brittain and Rakiya Omaar - contributors - Basil Davidson/ Augustin Ndahimana Buranga/ Kathurima M'Inoti/ Lucy Hannan/ Jenny Matthews/ Ngugi Wa Mirii/ Kevin Watkins/ Joseph Hanlon/ Laurence Cockcroft/ Joseph Warioba/ Vic Allen and James Motlasi. Plus Bill Schwarz/ Wendy Wheeler/ Dave Featherstone.

Issue 8 - Active Welfare - editor Andrew Cooper - contributors - Rachel Hetherington and Helen Morgan/ John Pitts/ Angela Leopold/ Hassan Ezzedine/ Alain Grevot/ Margherita Gobbi/ Angelo Cassin and Monica Savio. Plus Michael Rustin/ Colette Harris/ Patrick Wright.

Issue 9 - European Left - editor Martin Peterson - contributors - Branka Likic-Brboric/ Mate Szabo/ Leonadis Donskis/ Peter Weinreich/ Alain Caille/ John Crowley/ Ove

Sernhede and Alexandra Alund. Plus Angela McRobbie/ Mario Petrucci/ Philip Arestis and Malcolm Sawyer.

Issue 10 - Windrush Echoes - editors Gail Lewis and Lola Young - contributors - Anne Phoenix/ Jackie Kay/ Julia Sudbury/ Femi Franklin/ David Sibley/ Mike Phillips/ Phil Cole/ Bilkis Malek/ Sonia Boyce/ Roshi Naidoo/ Val Wilmer and Stuart Hall. Plus Alan Finlayson/ Richard Moncrieff/ Mario Pianta.

Issue 11 - Emotional Labour - editor Pam Smith - contributors - Stephen Lloyd Smith/ Dympna Casey/ Marjorie Mayo/ Minoo Moallem/ Prue Chamberlayne/ Rosy Martin/ Sue Williams and Gillian Clarke. Plus Andreas Hess/ T. V. Sathyamurthy/ Les Black, Tim Crabbe and John Solomos.

Issue 12 - Transversal Politics - editors Cynthia Cockburn and Lynette Hunter - contributors - Nira Yuval-Davis/ Pragna Patel/ Marie Mulholland/ Rebecca O'Rourke/ Gerri Moriarty/ Jane Plastow and Rosie. Plus Bruno Latour/ Gerry Hassan/ Nick Jeffrey.

Issue 13 - These Sporting Times - editor Andrew Blake - contributors - Carol Smith/ Simon Cook/ Adam Brown/ Steve Greenfield/ Guy Osborne/ Gemma Bryden/ Steve Hawes/ Alan Tomlinson and Adam Locks. Plus Geoff Andrews/ Fred Halliday/ Nick Henry and Adrian Passmore.

Issue 14 - One-Dimensional Politics - editors Wendy Wheeler and Michael Rustin - contributors - Wendy Wheeler/ Michael Rustin/ Dave Byrne/ Gavin Poynter/ Barry Richards and Mario Petrucci. Plus Ann Briggs/ David Renton/ Isaac Balbus/ Laura Dubinsky.

Issue 15 - States of Mind - contributors - Alan Shuttleworth/ Andrew Cooper/ Helen Lucey/ Diane Reay/ Richard Graham and Jennifer Wakelyn. Plus Nancy Fraser/ Stephen Wilkinson/ Mike Waite/ Kate Young.

Issue 16 - Civil Society - editor Andreas Hess - contributors - Jeffrey C. Alexander/ Robert Fine/ Maria Pia Lara/ William Outhwaite/ Claire Wallace/ Grazyna Kubica-Heller/ Jonathan Freedland. Plus Peter Howells/ G. C.Harcourt/ Emma Satyamurti/ Simon Lewis/ Paulette Goudge/ Tom Wengraf.

Issue 17 - New Political Directions - contributors - Sarah Benton/ Giulio Marcon and Mario Pianta/ Massimo Cacciari/ Sue Tibballs/ Richard Minns/ Ian Taylor/ John Calmore/ Judith Rugg and Michele Sedgwick/ Ruby Millington/ Merilyn Moos/ Jon Bloomfield/ Nick Henry/ Phil Hubbard/ Kevin Ward and David Donnison.

Issue 18 - A Very British Affair - editor Gerry Hassan - contributors - Gerry Hassan/ Jim McCormick/ Mark Perryman/ Katie Grant/ Cathal McCall/ Charlotte Williams/ Paul Chaney/ John Coakley/ Kevin Howard/ Mary-Ann Stephenson/ David T. Evans. Plus Hilary Wainwright/ Angie Birtill/ Beatrix Campbell/ Jane Foot and Csaba Deak/ Geoff Andrews/ Glyn Ford/ Jane Desmarais.

Issue 19 - New World Disorder - contributors Stuart Hall/ Chantal Mouffe/ Gary Younge/ Eli Zaretsky/ David Slater/ Bob Hackett. Plus Jonathan Rutherford/ Anne Costello/ Les Levidow/ Linda McDowell.

Issue 20 - Regimes of Emotion - editors Pam Smith and Stephen Lloyd Smith - contributors - Pam Smith/ Steve Smith/ Arlie Russell Hochschild/ Fiona Douglas/ Maria Lorentzon/ Gay Lee/ Del Loewenthal/ David Newbold/ Bridget Towers/ Stuart Nairn/ Rick Rattue/ Nelarine Cornelius/ Ian Robbins/ Marjorie Mayo/ Trudi James. Plus Nira Yuval Davis, Haim Bresheeth, Lena Jayyusi/ Anita Biressi and Heather Nunn/ Andrew Stevens/ John Grieve Smith & G.C. Harcourt/ Fraser Mcdonald & Andy Cumbers.

Issue 21 - Monsters and Morals - editor Elizabeth B. Silva - contributors - Elizabeth Silva/ Paul Dosh/ Margrit Shildrick/ Janet Fink/ Dale Southerton/ Caroline Knowles. Plus Geoff Andrews/ Tom Kay/ Richard Minns/ Steve Woodhams.

Issue 22 - Fears and Hopes - Irene Bruegel/ Tom Kay/ Paddy Maynes/ Sarah Whatmore and Steve Hinchliffe/ Stuart Hall/ Chantal Mouffe/ Ernesto Laclau/ Geoff Andrews/ Stefan Howald/ David Renton.

Issue 23 - Who needs history? - Geoff Andrews/ Kevin Morgan/ Ilaria Favretto/ John Callaghan/ Maud Bracke and Willie Thompson/ plus Michael Rustin/ Ali Ansari/ Costis Hadjimichalis and Ray Hudson/ Christian Wolmar/ Alan Finlayson/ C. Harcourt/ Laura Agustín.

Issue 24 - A market state? - Stuart Hall/ Alan Finlayson/ Jonathan Rutherford/ Richard Minns/ Renzio Imbeni/ George Irvin/ Adah Kay/ Nora Räthzel/ Michael Saward/ Nora Carlin/ Michael Rustin.

Issue 25 - Rocky times - Geoff Andrews/ Alan Fountain/ Ivor Gaber/ Ash Amin, Doreen Massey, Nigel Thrift/ Gerry Hassan/ Hugh Mackay/ Francisco Domínguez//George Irvin/ Grahame Thompson.

All back issues cost £9.99, postfree. Order from Soundings, Lawrence & Wishart, 99a Wallis Road, London E9 5LN or email to soundings@lwbooks.co.uk. Tel: 020 8533 2506 Fax: 020 8533 7369

Soundings

Described by the political theorist John Gray as a 'well written and welcome journal', Soundings *is a unique venture that combines hard-edged political argument with a broad spectrum of cultural content. Highlights have included Stuart Hall, Jackie Kay, Gail Lewis, Mike Phillips and Lola Young on the significance of Windrush; Victoria Brittain and Basil Davidson on states of Africa; Chantal Mouffe on the third way; Angela McRobbie on the culture industries; and Bill Schwarz on the Tories; special themes have also included the* European Left, Young Britain, One-Dimensional Politics *and* A Very British Affair.

SPECIAL OFFER TO NEW SUBSCRIBERS

First time individual subscribers are entitled to a
£30 subscription for the first year

Subscription rates 2004 (3 issues)

Individual subscriptions: *UK* £35.00   *Rest of the World* £45

Institutional subscriptions: *UK* £70.00   *Rest of the World* £80.00

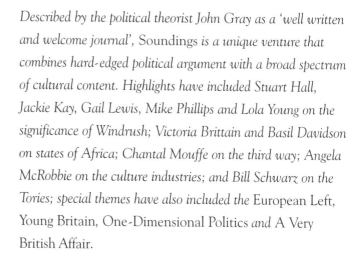

To subscribe, send your name and address and payment (cheque or credit card), stating which issue you want the subscription to start with, to Soundings, Lawrence and Wishart, 99a Wallis Road, London E9 5LN.
OR you can e-mail us at
subscriptions@l-w-bks.demon.co.uk